A Shining Lamp

A Shining Lamp

The Oral Instructions of Catherine McAuley

Mary C. Sullivan, RSM, Editor

The Catholic University of America Press
Washington, D.C.

The paper used in this publication meets the minimum requirements of American National Standards for Information Science—Permanence of Paper for Printed Library Materials, ANSI Z39.48–1984.
∞

Cataloging-in-Publication Data available from the Library of Congress
ISBN 978-0-8132-2926-3

Contents

Preface

The spoken and written words of many inspiring women and men have often been lost to later generations for the simple reason that no one gathered up their words and preserved them. Happily, the early companions of Catherine McAuley (1778–1841)—Sisters of Mercy who loved her and treasured her guidance—were good scribes and archivists.

Their full-time work was not writing or safeguarding historical records, but teaching poor girls in schoolrooms all across Ireland and parts of England, sheltering and providing employment training for homeless women and girls, and visiting the sick and dying poor in their hovels in back alleys. Yet alongside these daily works of mercy, spiritual and corporal, they also somehow managed to record, as best they could, Catherine's oral advice to them, her frequent sayings, even her anecdotes and humorous remarks, and to preserve her many letters, poems, and other writings.

For their generous legacy to the worldwide Mercy family and to all the people of God—a legacy partly shared in this book—I can only express my deep gratitude and respect. Those who have ever tried to write something in between the cracks the days allow will surely understand Mary Clare Moore's apology for her "scribbling," when her hand was tired, and her regret that she "could not write more today."

To these early Mercy women who showed such care for what

was to them an unknown future, I dedicate this book of Catherine McAuley's oral instructions. They are its true scribes and editors.

To all the early and present-day Mercy archivists who have preserved these documents, especially Marianne Cosgrave at Mercy Congregational Archives, Dublin, and to Louise Novros, who so expertly and patiently prepared the manuscript for this book, I offer my sincere thanks and admiration. This book could not have happened without their help.

I have chosen to title the book *A Shining Lamp: The Oral Instructions of Catherine McAuley* because that metaphor may suggest a helpful way to view its contents. In her instructions Catherine says that "we should be shining lamps giving light to all around us." She apparently had in mind Jesus' saying in Matthew's Gospel: "No one after lighting a lamp puts it under the bushel basket, but on the lampstand, and it gives light to all in the house. In the same way, let your light shine before others, so that they may see your good works and give glory to your Father in heaven" (5:15–16).

Catherine knew full well that any light that might be shining in her lamp came not from her, but from the one truly efficacious Lamplighter, Jesus Christ, "the light of the world" (John 8:12). For her, the effect that surrendering to the light of the Gospel "should produce is to render you as a lamp consumed with the fire of divine love, shining and giving light to all."

When Catherine McAuley died in November 1841, the grieving Mary Ann Doyle, her earliest Mercy coworker, called her "a light to one's feet" and a "stay and encouragement . . . in the everyday difficulties and perplexities of life." May some word of Catherine's, something she once said, be such a light and encouragement for those who read this book.

Abbreviations

Compilations of Primary Sources

CMcATM — Mary C. Sullivan, *Catherine McAuley and the Tradition of Mercy* (Dublin: Four Courts Press, 1995; Notre Dame, Ind.: University of Notre Dame Press, 1995). Texts of biographical manuscripts and letters about Catherine McAuley written by her contemporaries; the original Rule and Constitutions of the Sisters of Mercy, which she composed; and excerpts from the annals of two early Mercy communities.

CCMcA — Mary C. Sullivan, ed., *The Correspondence of Catherine McAuley, 1818–1841* (Dublin: Four Courts Press, 2004; Washington, D.C.: The Catholic University of America Press, 2004).

PS — [Mary Clare Moore, comp.,] *The Practical Sayings of Catherine McAuley* (London: Burns, Oates, 1868); reprint, Mary C. Sullivan, ed. (Rochester, N.Y.: Sisters of Mercy of the Americas, 2010).

Archives

AIMGB — Archives, Institute of Our Lady of Mercy, Bermondsey, London

ASMBNI — Archives, Congregation of the Sisters of Mercy (Northern Province), Bessbrook, Northern Ireland

ASMSJN — Archives, Sisters of Mercy, St. John's, Newfoundland

AUSMGB — Archives, Union of Sisters of Mercy Great Britain, Handsworth, Birmingham

MCA — Mercy Congregational Archives, Dublin

MHCSMA — Mercy Heritage Center, Institute of the Sisters of Mercy of the Americas, Belmont, North Carolina

Part 1

Introduction

The Second Vatican Council (1962–65) invited each religious congregation to engage in "a continuous return to the sources of all Christian life and to the original inspiration behind a given community." This invitation urged religious to focus, not once but continuously, on the "following of Christ as proposed by the gospel" as their "fundamental norm," and to accord "loyal recognition and safekeeping ... to the spirit of founders" and "the particular goals and wholesome traditions which constitute the heritage of each community."[1]

Whatever fidelity the Sisters of Mercy of the world may have had to the Gospel and to the spirit of Catherine McAuley (1778–1841) prior to 1965—and in many respects this seems to have been remarkably strong—their efforts to hold fast to these precious realities have only deepened and strengthened over the last fifty years. Catherine had often assured them that such fidelity was God's work, and that "if we are humble and sincere, God will finish in us the work God has begun."[2] This work of God is not yet "finished" in the sense of "completed" or "ended." It will be in process until the day when the Christ in the last Sister of Mercy may be able to say for her: "It is finished" (John 19:30).

The purpose of the present book is not to describe directly the efforts that Sisters of Mercy and their partners in ministry have made and will continue to make to "return" to and embrace the Gospel—as unfailingly primary as such an endeavor has been and must be. Rather its aim is humbler: to offer scholars in a variety of fields as well as Sisters of Mercy, their friends, associates, companions, coworkers, and other Christians further insights—using her own words of instruction—into the original inspiration of Catherine McAuley and her understanding of the Christian and religious life.

Her inspiration and understanding were gifts of God, what St. Paul calls charisms. Charisms are always given for the sake of others. They are helps that God gives to a person or a community to enable that person or community to carry out the mission, the Gospel tasks, God has asked of them. Every religious congregation, as indeed the whole Church, hopes that the charisms of the founder may also be granted to the followers. Catherine herself was confident of this; as she once wrote, God "never calls any person … for any end without giving the means and necessary helps to carry them through all the difficulties of it. … We ought then have great confidence in God in the discharge of all these offices of mercy, spiritual and corporal—which constitute the business of our lives."[3]

The Manuscript Compilation, Its Sources, and Its Archetypes

The research that underlies the present volume has attempted to get as close as possible to the original language of the oral instructions Catherine McAuley gave to the first Sisters of Mercy in the decade 1831–41, from the founding of the congregation on

December 12, 1831, to her death on November 11, 1841. In those years numerous Retreat Sundays, annual retreats, and retreats prior to ceremonies for the reception of new novices or their profession of religious vows took place at Baggot Street, Dublin, in the first Mercy convent. During these days or weeks of spiritual reflection on the religious character of their lives, Catherine personally provided most if not all of the related instructions—either through her own composed and spoken words or through her oral presentation of content she had chosen from previously published spiritual works.

Part 2 is, therefore, the most important section of this book: the exact text of the manuscript compilation (193 handwritten pages) titled "Instructions of Revd. Mother M. Catherine McAuley, the Ven[erated] Foundress of The Religious [called] Sisters of Mercy, 1832–3–4." Mary Bertrand Degnan, RSM, used this manuscript—which is preserved in the Mercy Congregational Archives (MCA), Dublin—but routinely altered it (occasionally in only minor ways) for her publication, *Retreat Instructions of Mother Mary Catherine McAuley* (Westminster, Md.: Newman Press, 1952). Not included in part 2 is the manuscript's "Index" (that is, table of contents) or its lengthy "Introduction, By a Sister of the Institute" which Degnan (pages 16–23) ascribed—I believe, incorrectly—to Mary Teresa Purcell and extensively altered, using only about half of its original wording.[4]

I have chosen to present the text of this particular manuscript for several reasons. It is a compilation of several of Catherine's oral instructions given in the 1830s, and as such is the longest and evidently the earliest such compilation (having possibly been completed in the early 1850s or before).[5] Moreover, the individual sections of this long manuscript also exist in what are, presumably, even earlier manuscripts attributable to Catherine's contemporaries at Baggot Street. These shorter manuscripts of "instructions," which I call *archetypes,* are generally identical or nearly identical to the wording in the corresponding sections of the compiled manuscript presented in part 2. This fact strengthens the authenticity of that long manuscript as a faithful—insofar as humanly possible—albeit secondhand, record of some of Catherine's actual oral instructions.

Two possible traps threaten the composition of an introduction like this one: attempting to explain too much, and not saying enough. I hope I have generally avoided both. If I have failed, the reader is of course free at any point to move on to part 2.

Thus two kinds of previously composed material are related to Catherine McAuley's instructions as presented in part 2 of this volume. The first kind is previously published spiritual books that function as *sources* on which Catherine frequently relied for the wording or content in her instructions. The second kind is the manuscript *archetypes* to which I have just referred and which will be discussed at length later in this introduction.

Catherine used her *sources,* that is, passages from previously published books by certain spiritual writers, in at least three ways. She sometimes quoted from them directly; she often paraphrased their content; and where her instructions appear to have no direct dependence on the wording of a particular spiritual writer, her expressed thoughts, values, and concerns nonetheless seem influenced by that published account. This influence is especially evident in her long and frequent instructions on charity, humility, poverty of spirit, obedience, and the passion and death of Jesus Christ.

The work of finding the previously published spiritual books on whose wording or general content Catherine McAuley may have relied as she prepared and then gave oral instructions to the first Sisters of Mercy has involved repeatedly searching for needles in haystacks. The search was initially limited to considering only the published spiritual works (in English translation) that Catherine is known to have read, either on her own or to the Baggot Street community. The following titles are all mentioned in the early biographical manuscripts written about her by her contemporaries: Alonso Rodriguez, SJ (1526–1616), *The Practice of Christian and Religious Perfection;*[6] Abbé Barthélémy Baudrand, SJ (1701–87), *Elevation of the Soul to God* and *The Soul on Calvary;* John Gother (–1704), *The Sinner's Complaints to God;*[7] Thomas à Kempis (1380?–1471), *The Imitation of Christ;*[8] Francis Blyth, ODC (1705?–72), *A Devout Paraphrase on the Seven Penitential Psalms;* Luis de Granada (1504–88), *The Sinner's Guide;* Richard Challoner (1691–1781), *A Journal of Meditations for Every Day in the Year;* Alphonsus Liguori (1696–1787), *Visits to the Most Holy Sacrament;* Alban Butler (1710–73), *Lives of the Saints;* and Ursula Young, OSU (1783–1830), *The Soul United to Jesus.*

Each of these titles was published in numerous editions. The titles originally published in French, Spanish, or Italian were frequently translated into English language editions, often with varying English titles. In this study I have, in each case, consulted an English edition that Catherine McAuley is known to have used or one that was published before or during her time, or close to it. Chief among these books, in providing wording for Catherine's instructions, was Rodriguez's three-volume work, but one also finds in some of the other works listed above many passages that may have influenced Catherine's wording or thinking. Where appropriate, references will appear in the notes to part 2.

The search for *sources* was then extended to other published works with which, from a variety of circumstantial evidence, one can reasonably conclude that Catherine McAuley was familiar. In fact, exact or nearly exact quotations from two of them appear in the "instructions" presented in part 2. The language of Louis Bourdaloue, SJ (1632–1704), *Spiritual Retreat for Religious Persons* (1828 edition), is quoted in several places, sometimes at length, as well as in the *archetypes* of those sections. The thoughts of Michel-Ange Marin (1697–1767), *The Perfect Religious,* appear occasionally.[9] References to Bourdaloue's and Marin's works will be given in the notes to part 2.

Transcriptions of parts of Jean-Pierre Camus (1584–1652), *The Spirit of St. Francis de Sales,* and John Grou, SJ (1731–1803), *Spiritual Maxims,* are preserved in the Dublin archival collection. Since these transcriptions were probably made by some of Catherine McAuley's earliest associates, these published books have also been examined, but so far to no avail. Alphonsus Liguori's *The Nun Sanctified, or, The True Spouse of Jesus Christ* was also considered, since published copies of it and transcriptions of parts of it exist in many of the earliest Mercy archives. But, here again, no direct correspondences with its wording or exact content have so far been discovered in Catherine's "instructions" as presented in part 2.

Earlier in this introduction I referred to *archetypes,* that is, to manuscripts that, in fact, closely correspond, in wording and content, to sections of the manuscript compilation presented in part 2. These earlier manuscripts, written prior to that compilation (and later transcriptions of them, such as the compilation itself) can be found in the archival collections of many of the earliest Mercy convents. They were originally handwritten by Mercy women who actually listened to Catherine's instructions and who may have written notes as she spoke, copied manuscript transcripts taken from her *sources,* and finally attempted to set down not only the main points of her instructions, but also, and insofar as humanly possible, her personal expansions of those points. Exactly how they assembled and/or recorded her instructions seems, to this researcher, presently impossible to ascertain with confidence.

Subsequent transcribers of these original archetypal manuscripts sometimes used paraphrasing, not always copying the original word for word. But since they understood that they were dealing with the instructions "of the foundress," who was revered while she lived and long after her death, they apparently strove to be as faithful as they could to the content and wording they saw in the manuscripts before them. Thus a remarkable measure of identity, in both content and wording, characterizes the various *archetypes* and later transcriptions of them, including the compilation presented in part 2, as well as between some of the *archetypes* themselves.

The original manuscripts that I consider to be *archetypes* of the compilation can all be traced—either by the name associated with the manuscript, the handwriting, or the archival location—to the following Sisters of Mercy whom Catherine McAuley instructed at Baggot Street in the decade 1831–41, and on more than one occasion: Mary Ann Doyle, Mary Clare Moore, Mary Frances Warde, Mary Teresa Purcell, Mary Juliana Hardman, Mary Liguori Gibson, and Mary Francis Creedon.

To this list of manuscript writers must be added Catherine McAuley herself, since two manuscripts in her hand also correspond, in content and wording, to portions of the instructions presented in part 2. These are her hand-printed manuscript on various spiritual topics, including the spirit of the Gospel and the maxims of Jesus Christ, and her transcription—apparently made during her 1830–31 novitiate in the Presentation Convent on

George's Hill, Dublin—of chapters from the first three treatises in volume one of Rodriguez's *Practice of Christian and Religious Perfection* (1806 edition).

All these archetypal manuscripts or later transcriptions thereof can be found in the archival collections of Mercy convents closely related to their presumably original scribes—that is, the collections of Dublin, Derry, and Naas in Ireland; Bermondsey (London), Birmingham, and Liverpool in England; Manchester, New Hampshire (USA); and St. John's in Newfoundland. Wherever in part 2 portions of these *archetypes* seem to underlie the wording or content of long passages of the manuscript compilation, this fact will be cited in the notes.

Thus, in view of their close relationship to the *archetypes,* the "instructions" presented in part 2 can be truly said to be some of the oral instructions Catherine McAuley gave to the first Sisters of Mercy. While she did not compose all the words contained therein, she probably did orally compose many of them, especially her more colloquial comments on certain topics, her claims about what certain scripture passages do not say, some of the questions she addressed to her hearers, and some of the homely images and illustrations she inserted in the passages taken from or influenced by previously published *sources.*

In the compilation one also frequently encounters nearly exact wording to many passages of *A Little Book of Practical Sayings, Advices and Prayers of . . . Mary Catharine* [*sic*] *McAuley,* a booklet Mary Clare Moore compiled and published in London in 1868. These "sayings" occur especially in chapters 1 (27 passages) and 5 (27 passages) of the compilation. They also occur in Bermondsey Manuscript IOLM/BER/12/1/4, which serves as a nearly identical *archetype* of most of chapter 1 and of sections of chapter 5. At present, that Bermondsey manuscript cannot be confidently dated, nor can its handwriting be confidently identified. However, given that the "sayings" in the "instructions" (part 2) follow in the same sequence as they appear in the Bermondsey manuscript, it seems clear that this manuscript preceded the 1868 publication of the *Practical Sayings.* As Clare Moore, the compiler of the *Practical Sayings,* says in the Bermondsey Annals for 1868: "One of the resolutions ... which followed the August Retreat this year was a determination to collect even a few of the maxims and practical sayings of our revered Foundress.... The Bishop [of Southwark, Thomas Grant] recommended to have the Maxims classified under different heads: Humility, Charity, etc., with references to the chapters of our Rule which they served to illustrate."[10] Hence, in the "instructions" (part 2), Catherine McAuley's sayings are not in the order in which they appear in the 1968 publication, but follow in the order in which they originally appeared in Bermondsey Manuscript IOLM/BER/12/1/4, preserved in AIMGB.

When Catherine gave oral instructions to the Sisters of Mercy, what she said to them was not entirely extempore. Apparently she read some of her instructions, either directly from the published books that were her *sources* or from inexact handwritten transcriptions of parts of those books. However, she did not confine herself to the printed or handwritten words before her. In the compilation, one frequently notices what must have been moments when she looked up from the page—injecting her own thoughts, questions, metaphors, teasing anecdotes, expansions of the text she had just read, or interpretive comments on scriptural passages. In these moments her words were realistic, practical, homespun, and at times even outright playful. She was a teacher, with a book or notebook in her hand, not simply an undeviating reader of words on a page. Here one can see the truth of Mary Clare Moore's claim: she "loved simplicity singularly in others, and practised it herself, telling the Sisters to adopt a simple style of speaking and writing.... Even in piety she disliked highflown aspirations or sentences."[11]

As Clare says in the biography of Catherine in the Bermondsey Annals (1841), and Mary Vincent Harnett repeats in the Limerick Manuscript:

> She had an extensive knowledge of the human heart, and could readily adapt her conversation to the wants of those by whom she was surrounded. Her method of reading was so delightful that all used to acknowledge it rendered quite new to them a subject which perhaps they had frequently heard before, for she considered it most useful to adhere to a few solid spiritual works, rather than to run over many without reflection.[12]

Clare says that Catherine's lectures were "half an hour in the morning, and half an hour in the evening" and that they were "most animated and impressive, especially on the duties of charity and humility." She also notes that Catherine "loved to expatiate on certain words."[13]

The Tullamore Annals for 1836, in which Mary Ann Doyle had a voice, says: "The eloquence that flowed from her lips when instructing the sisters, especially for making their Vows, went straight to their hearts.... Her language was simple and unstudied, but sweet and forcible; it was the fruit of prayer, and the sisters seemed impressed with the idea that whatever she inculcated was the holy will of God for them to do."[14]

Sorting out the history and the early texts of what can be reasonably called "Catherine McAuley's oral instructions" is, admittedly, complicated, both for the present-day reader of her instructions and for any researcher. But without some extensive attempt to examine the existing manuscripts and their *sources* and *archetypes*, it is difficult to claim that we truly have in hand, as reliably as possible, Catherine's actual instructions, and not simply later words ascribed to her without sufficient warrant. I am confident that the manuscript compilation presented in part 2 of this volume fulfills this hope.

The Attitudes and Characteristics of Catherine's Instructions

Catherine McAuley can surely speak for herself and has obviously done so in the "instructions" presented in part 2. But since her instructions to the first Sisters of Mercy were so extensive—appearing not only in the manuscript compilation presented in this book, but also in her many letters, poems, and other writings—it might be helpful to note Catherine's personal attitudes toward her task of instructing, as well as certain general characteristics of her instructions.

Basically, over the decade of the 1830s, Catherine did her best to articulate a spirituality of merciful living inspired by the Gospel and the existing understanding of vowed religious life. But she was always conscious that she herself had much to learn in this regard. She never claimed that she and the Sisters of Mercy had completely grasped the full meaning and implications of apostolic religious life or had achieved thoroughgoing fidelity to what Christ asked of them. In January 1839 she was well aware that "we have been deficient enough, and far, very far, from co-operating generously with God in our regard, but we will try to do better—all of us." Later that year she admitted, "The adage—'never too old to learn'—is a great comfort to me." She was then sixty-one. Even in April 1841, seven months before her death, she wrote to her old companion Frances Warde, "our experience in religious life has been so short that a good faithful Sister to whom

God has imparted grace may be said to know as much of spiritual life as we do."[15]

Consequently, Catherine's instructions—for example, her strong emphases on "resemblance" to Jesus Christ, union and charity, humility of mind and heart, cheerful acceptance of "portions of the Cross," and confidence in the accompanying providence of God—are best understood when we keep the honesty and humility of the teacher in mind. She knew that she was also addressing herself and that if she listened to herself, she too might grow in fidelity, for, as she said, "those who instruct others improve themselves by the very act. That which we say to and for others cannot but regard ourselves."[16] In no sense did Catherine see herself as adequately equipped to guide and teach the first Sisters of Mercy, let alone those she never imagined would be living in the twenty-first century. Yet despite this self-assessment, she apparently felt a personal responsibility to do all she could to contribute to their formation. While their faithful following of Christ was wholly God's work, it also required effort on her part. That was the fundamental Gospel paradox: the great "as if" of human effort. As she once wrote: "While we place all our confidence in God, we must act as if all depended on our exertion."[17]

So Catherine exerted herself, to learn what she should share with others. She studied, read available books, and apparently tried to listen to what God was teaching her. All her early colleagues in the Sisters of Mercy acknowledge this. Mary Vincent Harnett says that "she did not possess worldly accomplishments, but she had read much and well." Clare Moore says that at Baggot Street, even before the founding of the congregation, Catherine with one or two others used to rise at four in the morning to pray "the whole of her favorite Psalter [of Jesus] and read some spiritual book."[18] Mary Clare Augustine Moore recounts Catherine's reading to the community from *The Sinner's Complaints*, *The Elevation of the Soul*, and *The Sufferings of Christ*, works by, respectively, John Gother, Barthélémy Baudrand, and Thomas of Jesus or Baudrand.[19]

Though Catherine never spoke of herself as the "founder" of the Sisters of Mercy or acted as if she thought of herself in that way—a Carlow novice remarked on the "total absence of everything in her manner telling, I am the foundress"[20]—she took to heart what she perceived to be her obligations as the one whom Dublin Archbishop Daniel Murray insisted on calling the "Mother Superior." She tried to become "a pattern to the community."[21] She knew that, at least initially, she would have to be the only Mistress of Novices they had. She would have to "form those under her care in humility and solid virtue," enable them to become "truly sensible of the end they should have in view," help them to "unite their hearts perfectly to God by dying to themselves," and instruct them in all the ways laid out in the long chapter of the Rule on the formation of the novices.[22] Actually, she would have preferred to remain a novice herself, rather than be the superior. She often said that "during no time of her life was she so happy as when a novice" in the Presentation Convent, "and were she permitted to have a choice it would be to continue always living under obedience, rather than to have the government of others."[23]

Ignatian Influences

A strongly Ignatian spirituality underlies much of the thought and emphasis in Catherine's instructions. This comes as no surprise given what we will discover about Catherine's extensive reliance in her instructions as presented in part 2 on books by Alonso Rodriguez, SJ, and Louis Bourdaloue, SJ, whether that reliance appears in her exact wording, her paraphrases, or the general tenor of her thought. One of the most remarkable uses Catherine made of Rodriguez's *Practice of Christian and Religious Perfection* (Kilkenny: John Reynolds, 1806) was her transformation of the wording in about half of his treatise "On the End for Which the Society of Jesus Was Instituted—the Means Which Are Conducive to This End ..." (vol. 3:3–92) into her essay on "The Spirit of the Institute [of Mercy]."[24]

Moreover, two additional books that Catherine is known to have read to the Baggot Street community in translation were also written by a Jesuit: Abbe Barthélémy Baudrand (1701–87). His books, *Elevation of the Soul to God* and *Soul on Calvary,* contain the same spiritual understandings and emphases that one finds in Catherine's instructions as presented in part 2. In addition to these influences, one of her earliest spiritual advisors, until his death in 1811, was Thomas Betagh, a Jesuit priest who continued to work in Dublin in the years following the papal suppression of the Society of Jesus in 1773. Clare Moore says that Catherine "went often" to him "for instruction," for his "learning and piety made every one revere his words."[25]

Many elements of Ignatian spirituality, as represented by these Jesuit authors and possibly by Betagh's advice, are revealed in Catherine's instructions. We see this in her comments on humility, charity toward one's neighbor, love of God, obedience, poverty of spirit, self-denial, apostolic self-bestowal, conformity to the will of God, detachment from and indifference toward earthly things, and the nature of prayer—all culminating in her focus on the humanity, virtues, and passion and death of Jesus Christ. This list of spiritual themes is only suggestive; it cannot do justice to the thinking of St. Ignatius Loyola or Catherine McAuley. It simply points, in brief form, to some of the Ignatian topics and concerns that reappear in Catherine's instructions to the first Sisters of Mercy. Like that of St. Ignatius, Catherine's was an ascetical and moral spirituality in service of the Gospel: a deeply Christian and religious practice that strove to resemble and follow the example of Jesus Christ, relying on God's mercy and unfailing providence.

Teresian Influences

Catherine's instructions to the first generation of the Sisters of Mercy also exhibit a distinctly Teresian spirituality. As one reads her words one hears thoughts and emphases that are very similar to those of Teresa of Avila. How Catherine came to know the teachings of St. Teresa is not fully known. Yet if one reads the biographies and spiritual writings of these two women, their lives separated by over 250 years, one can easily conclude that they were kindred personalities and shared a comparable understanding of the essence of the spiritual and religious life. The one exception may perhaps involve their personal experience of prayer, though that is not certain.[26]

This Teresian influence is understandable, given the early history of the Sisters of Mercy. The religious congregation in Dublin who did the most to support the early lay community on Baggot Street from 1827 on, and then the new religious congregation into which it evolved in 1831, was the Discalced Carmelite Friars at St. Teresa's Church on Clarendon Street. In the beginning they presided at Eucharists on Baggot Street and supplied all the materials needed for those celebrations. In June 1829 their prior, Redmond O'Hanlon, became the confessor of the community, a post he fulfilled until his death in 1864. When, in 1829–30, Catherine and her coworkers contemplated founding a new religious congregation devoted to the works of mercy, the Carmelite Friars on Clarendon Street, including Redmond O'Hanlon and Francis L'Estrange, gave them a copy of the Teresian Rule and evidently urged them to accept the offer of affiliation as a Third Order with the Carmelite nuns on Warren-mount in Dublin. These Carmelite women, though observing enclosure, also conducted a school for poor girls.

After the founding of the Sisters of Mercy in December 1831, until Archbishop Daniel Murray's death in 1852, Redmond O'Hanlon apparently also served as the archbishop's deputy with respect to the governance of the congregation. Consequently, throughout the decade of the 1830s, he was not only Catherine's confessor but also her helper and uniformly self-effacing confidant. He accompanied her on several trips to found additional Mercy convents; he visited these foundations when she could not, and quietly urged her to take care of her health; and he arranged that the first thirteen Sisters of Mercy to die in Dublin were interred in the Carmelite burial vault at St. Teresa's on Clarendon Street. In the end he anointed Catherine, celebrated her requiem, and assisted in her burial in the newly consecrated cemetery at the convent on Baggot Street. As she once wrote of him, "there scarcely ever was so disinterested a friend" of the Sisters of Mercy.[27]

In view of all this, it is not inconceivable that O'Hanlon gave Catherine and the Mercy community on Baggot Street books on Carmelite spirituality or by Carmelite authors. One of Catherine's favorite books was *A Devout Paraphrase on the Seven Penitential Psalms* by the French Discalced Carmelite Francis Blyth. It is also obvious that she knew and admired the life of Teresa of Avila. Once, while she was founding a community in Limerick, she asked Mary Teresa White (named after the saint) to "implore

Saint Teresa who loved foundations to intercede for poor Limerick where no seed has yet taken root"—that is, no convent of any religious order had so far lasted there.[28]

Earlier, when Catherine, Anna Maria Doyle, and Elizabeth Harley received the habit in the Presentation Convent, Dublin, prior to founding the Sisters of Mercy, "the names [initially] given to them were Teresa, Clare, and Angela." But Catherine, "reflecting that these Saints ... were all Foundresses of Religious Orders, was uneasy lest it might be thought she ranked herself with them," and therefore begged "that they might retain their own names with the addition of Mary, which was granted at their profession."[29] At the first Mercy reception ceremony at Baggot Street on January 23, 1832, Catherine apparently felt no such qualms; she allowed two new novices, her own niece Mary and Frances Warde, to take the names Mary Joseph Teresa[30] and Mary Frances Teresa, and other novices to take Mary Clare and Mary Angela.

Since Catherine read to the community each day a portion of Alban Butler's *Lives of the Saints,* knowledge of St. Teresa's life and teachings would have been fairly prevalent in the Baggot Street community (Butler's entry for St. Teresa, on October 15, is forty pages long). Therefore, in writing their biographical manuscripts about Catherine McAuley, both Clare Moore and Mary Vincent Harnett could easily associate the zeal of the saint of Avila with that of their own founder: "She felt all the value of a vocation" to religious life, "and sought to extend the blessing to very many. Like the glorious Saint Teresa, she never refused any Postulant for want of temporal means when it was at all possible to provide what was essential."[31]

Clearly Catherine had some familiarity with Teresa's *Foundations.* She may also have read *The Way of Perfection;* a partial transcript of sections of *The Way* is in the archives of the Bermondsey (London) community founded in 1839. No evidence suggests that Catherine ever read *The Interior Castle,* although certain sentences in her instructions as presented in part 2 sound very like Teresa's advice in that book. For example, Teresa's assurance that "The Lord doesn't look so much at the greatness of our works as at the love with which they are done"; her no-nonsense claim that "the devil gives us great desires so that we will avoid setting ourselves to the task at hand, serving our Lord in possible things, and instead be content with having desired the impossible"; and her insistence that her sisters should desire to "be occupied in prayer not for the sake of our enjoyment but so as to have this strength to serve." Thus "Martha and Mary must join together in order to show hospitality to the Lord and have him always present and not host Him badly by failing to give Him something to eat."[32]

Numerous other Teresian convictions and insights appear to have influenced the content of Catherine's instructions to her sisters. These can be seen in her emphasis on humility of mind and heart, on the value of doing ordinary things well and meditating on the humanity of Jesus Christ, and in her belief, like Teresa, that "the soul's progress does not lie in thinking much but in loving much."[33] As is evident throughout her instructions, Catherine also shared Teresa's dislike of gloominess and gloomy responses, even though she probably never said, as Teresa is reputed to have said: "God deliver me from frowning saints!"[34]

Scriptural Interpretation

Like other members of the English-speaking Catholic Church in the nineteenth century, Catherine would have used Bishop

Richard Challoner's revision of the Douay-Rheims Bible (an English version of the Bible that was a translation of the Latin Vulgate).[35] Though no Bible she actually personally used has so far been discovered, she would have found copious scriptural quotations in many other books she is known to have read: for instance, William A. Gahan's *Catholic Piety,* Joseph Joy Dean's *Devotions to the Sacred Heart of Jesus,* and *The Little Office of the Blessed Virgin Mary,* in addition to the other titles mentioned earlier in this introduction.

What is most interesting about Catherine's scriptural references is the freshness and ease with which she interweaves them, and occasionally asserts what Jesus did *not* say, as she reflects on what the Gospel writers say he said. Clare Moore recalls that "when instructing the Sisters" Catherine used to say, "If His blessed words ought to be reverenced by all, with what loving devotion ought the Religious impress them on her memory, and try to reduce them to practice."[36] One has the sense that St. Paul's prayer for the Colossians was profoundly happening in her: "Let the word of Christ dwell in you richly; teach and admonish one another in all wisdom; and with gratitude in your hearts sing ... spiritual songs to God" (Col. 3:16).

Reading Catherine McAuley's Instructions

While reading Catherine's instructions, one may encounter terms, advice, or admonitions that seem alien to present-day experiences and understandings of Christian spirituality and of the nature and obligations of consecrated religious life. This tension is understandable and to be expected. Catherine was a woman of the early nineteenth century who drew her spiritual insights from her advisors and from translations of spiritual books first published in the eighteenth or an earlier century. She could share with her sisters only what she herself understood, and she was of course not an infallible interpreter of the ways of God. This is not to imply that the history of Christian thought and practice always progresses, or that the understandings of the twenty-first century are, by definition and the sheer passage of time, more accurate or reliable than those of the eighteenth century. Nor is it to affirm the reverse: namely, that only in the past were Christian realities understood appropriately.

Rather, resolving any tension one might experience in reading Catherine's instructions today calls for what may be called a fusion of horizons[37]—that is, a mutual listening and critical questioning between Catherine and the present-day "hearer" of her instructions. This interchange calls for a generous willingness to dialogue with her and her text; to seek to get beneath the archaic words and concepts she sometimes uses to what they fundamentally say; to ask in what sense or in what way her advice still applies, or now needs correction, amplification, or qualification; and to consider whether and to what extent her words continue to speak to what may be truly perennial in Christian and vowed religious life. This fusion of horizons also invites the present-day reader to inform Catherine (if that is not too presumptuous a verb), to tell her about current understandings and perspectives, and to assess the extent to which these two views, two horizons, may be reconciled.

What is to be avoided are two absolute and contrary conclusions. The first is that Catherine cannot, by reason of her assumptions and historical placement, say anything relevant to us now. The second is its opposite: that everything she said must be observed now as she said it and understood it, and twenty-first century circumstances and realizations are irrelevant. Even Catherine, at some level, understood Christian realities differently in 1841 than she did in 1831.

No, what is called for is an openness to considering what may well be the basic wisdom of her instructions about those realities of the Christian life and apostolic religious life that she regarded as enduring, and a corresponding openness to considering revision of whatever present-day understandings may be implicated. Thus, her instructions invite honest thought and meditation.

After Catherine's death, Mary Teresa White, one of the earliest Sisters of Mercy, wrote of her: "There was something about her so kind yet so discerning that you would fancy she read your heart. If you came to speak to her on the most trifling matter, although occupied with the most important affairs, she would instantly lay all aside and give you any satisfaction in her power."[38] Similarly, in 1860 Mary Vincent Whitty, another early sister, wrote of Catherine: "She was so humble yet dignified, so playful and witty, yet reserved and charitable, so pious and strict, yet amiable and kind, but to me at least the climax of her attractions was that she was always the same, always ready to listen, to consider and to direct whenever applied to."[39] So perhaps the most beneficial approach to reading Catherine's instructions today is to think of this encounter as a mutual discerning, a listening to one another, and an amiable reading of each other's heart.

The "Instructor" Herself

Catherine believed that "we should do first what we would induce others to do" and that "the way to virtue and to piety is shorter by example than by precept."[40] She knew that the character of anyone's life will always speak louder than her words. Therefore she understood the secondary status of her words to the first Sisters of Mercy: secondary not only to the character of her own life, but, most of all, secondary to the only truly efficacious Word, the One in whom "we live and move and have our being" (Acts 17:28).

Thus even as she tried to instruct her companions as best she could, she also realized, in her mind and heart, the deeply subordinate nature of her role and advice: "What could be more contrary to Humility than to hear a Religious speak in an authoritative tone of voice, to give her opinion in a confident, decided manner, when she should consider her opinion as nothing and herself a nobody."[41] Yet the "live coal" of God's Word had, it seems, touched the mouth of this nobody, and her nothing, it may be said, spoke on God's behalf—even though she would never have imagined this, and saw herself only as "your ever affectionate M. C. McAuley."

Editorial Methods

Some preliminary comments on the editorial methods used may prove helpful in reading the compiled manuscript of Catherine McAuley's oral instructions. These comments address the following features of the text: spelling and capitalization; punctuation, sentence structure, and paragraphing; italics; obsolete words and bracketed words, including [*sic*]; dates; scriptural quotations; and endnotes.

The capitalization and spelling in the manuscript have been preserved even when the spelling of a given word varies in different sections of the text—e.g., "endeavor" and "endeavour"; "neighbor" and "neighbour"; "practice" and "practise"—or is now no longer used ("brethern"). These variations are undoubtedly due to the different composers or transcribers of the various archetypal manuscripts that were collected into the single manuscript. All ampersands have been spelled out, but "viz." and "etc." have usually been left.

The punctuation and sentence structure in the manuscript have been generally followed, although some commas, semicolons, and periods have been inserted and some paragraphing added where these alterations seem needed to clarify the sense of the text.

Most of the underlinings (used for emphasis in the manuscript) have been preserved in the form of italics, and no italics have been added. However, some of the underlinings may have been added by the original transcribers or by subsequent readers of the compiled manuscript or of the archetypal manuscripts on which it is based. To the extent that these underlinings are historical additions, they may not reflect emphases that Catherine McAuley herself gave during her instructions. Nearly all exclamation points are also preserved, with the same reservation as noted for the underlinings.

The exact wording of the compiled manuscript has been followed. Where the compiler or transcriber of the manuscript or a section thereof obviously failed to include or copy correctly a word or words needed for the sense of the passage, an appropriate word is inserted in square brackets. Where confusing wording appears in the text, [*sic*] is sometimes used, though rarely. In the few instances where a factual error appears, a correction is inserted in square brackets.

Certain words commonly used in the early nineteenth century are now less frequently used, or have a different meaning. For example, "want" (whether used as a verb or a noun) usually meant "lack," and "in fine" was frequently used to mean "in short." It was an expression used to sum up, or to introduce a general statement following several particular ones. The word "inequality" often meant "lack of due proportion," or "unequal treatment," or "unevenness"; "motion" was often used where "emotion" would be used today. Catherine used "condescend" to signify a voluntary, gracious recognition of equality and solidarity, not implying any superiority. For her "religion" usually refers to the state of vowed religious life.

The dates that Degnan introduced into her 1952 publication

of the "retreat instructions" have not been preserved. However, the dates that actually appear in the text of the manuscript (in its title and in chapters 2, 3 and 4)—the years 1832–34, and the days of July—have all been preserved, even though they constitute a historical problem if they are thought to be too closely tied to "retreat instructions" given in the days before the Mercy ceremonies of reception or profession of religious vows.

Reception ceremonies at Baggot Street, Dublin, where Catherine McAuley presided, occurred as follows: 1832—in January and October; 1833—in July and December; and 1834—in February, July, and October. In both 1833 and 1834, the July reception ceremonies occurred on July 3: in 1833, Mary de Chantal McCann and Mary Teresa Purcell were received on that day; and in 1834, Mary Cecilia Marmion, young Catherine McAuley (the founder's niece), and Martha Wallplate. Teresa Purcell was a recorder or transcriber of some of Catherine's instructions. However, the July dates given in those chapters of the compiled manuscript that purport to record Catherine's instructions as given prior to a reception ceremony are all after July 3. In chapter 2 (no year given) the given dates are July 4 through August 1; and in chapter 3 (1834), they are July 11 through July 30. Possibly the novices transcribed what they remembered, or had noted, of Catherine's instructions in the days after they received the habit, but exactly why they recorded the particular dates they did is unclear. Moreover, no profession ceremonies occurred at Baggot Street in 1832. In 1833 four sisters professed vows in January, and one in November, on her deathbed. In 1834, four sisters professed vows: two in February and two in October. Hence no profession ceremony in those years appears to correspond with the "July" instructions given in chapters 2 and 3 of the compilation. Nor do these dates match the dates of the "annual retreats" of the Dublin community in August of each year.

In 1836, Catherine McAuley, with Mary Ann Doyle and Mary Teresa Purcell, founded the Mercy Convent in Tullamore on April 21, and Catherine remained in Tullamore until May 30. On May 27, 1836, Teresa Purcell, the supposed (?) recorder (according to Degnan) of the compiled manuscript of "retreat instructions," professed her vows in the parish chapel in Tullamore. The Tullamore Annals claims that during Catherine McAuley's stay in Tullamore, she prepared Mary Teresa Purcell for profession and that notes of these lectures were carefully penned by Teresa. However, "1836" does not match any of the dates given in the manuscript compilation of Catherine's instructions presented in this volume. An existing manuscript (Derry MS 86), which may be Teresa Purcell's "notes" (or a transcript thereof), is an *archetype* for one section of the compilation, but these "notes" should not be thought to cover the whole, much longer compilation.

There were of course numerous other occasions when Catherine McAuley instructed postulants or novices at Baggot Street in preparation for their reception or profession of vows, but these occasions, in 1835–41, came after the dates given in the manuscript compilation (1832–34). We know that in Birr, prior to the reception ceremony there on May 20, 1841, Catherine gave instructions to the two postulants, and she probably assisted in giving instructions in other foundations when she was present prior to their ceremonies of reception and/or profession—for example, in Cork (1837), Limerick (1838), Bermondsey (1839), and Galway (1840). Existing manuscripts that may be "notes" made by sisters who participated in these later occasions appear to constitute *archetypes* for various sections of the compiled manuscript of Catherine's "instructions."

It is not possible to identify the exact version of the Bible that Catherine McAuley uses for the scriptural quotations in her oral instructions. In each case she is using either the wording she remembers or the wording she finds in the published book that serves as the *source* for her comment. In part 2 the scriptural quotations are exactly as they appear in the compiled manuscript. In parts 1 and 3 the New Revised Standard Version is used, unless the text is quoting Catherine McAuley's scriptural reference.

The handwritten manuscript compilation presented in part 2 is divided into five chapters. So as not to distract from the "voice" of Catherine McAuley in these instructions to the first Sisters of Mercy, the notes for these chapters are presented at the end of the book. A general discussion of the *archetypes* and previously published *sources* related to the content appears at the end of each chapter.

Part 2

Instructions of Revd. Mother M. Catherine McAuley

The Ven[erated] Foundress of The Religious (called)

Sisters of Mercy 1832–3–4

CHAPTER 1ST

On the Vows and Charity, or, The Love of God and our Neighbour

Come apart into a desert place and rest awhile. —Mark [6.31]

Our Blessed Saviour in instructing His Disciples did not call them to entire separation from creatures, but a more intimate union of the heart with God. It is an invitation to serve Him with great confidence, free from that slavish fear unworthy of a child of God and a Spouse of Jesus Christ. You should consider in this solitude your great unworthiness to be called to so intimate a union with your God and of having your petition granted "To live in the House of God all the days of your life."[1]

It is one of the great secrets of God's Providence why He makes choice of some to be in a particular manner united to Him (which is one of the greatest graces He could bestow) and leave[s] so many thousands in the world, of whom many would have made greater efforts and attain perfection. In calling you to this, He puts you in the direct way of accomplishing His designs in your regard, one of the principal being that you are to give glory to His Name, and this you are not only to do by the sanctification of your own soul, but also by attracting others to God by word and example, so that in all they see and hear of you they may be induced to say "Glory be to God."[2]

You should now enter on the way of God. He has conducted you nearly to the end of your Novitiate, continuing His special graces to you. You should then endeavour to know what are His ways. It is supposed that not all the distractions at prayer or neglect of duty would cause God to withhold His graces from a Religious so much as a departure from His ways. A Religious who would be considered the most active of the Community, who would get through a great deal of business, and do this with what is called fuss, would be departing from the ways of God, which are all peace and tranquility. The humble, quiet Religious who would not do half so much, but did all in a manner becoming her character as a Religious would attract the eye of God far more and draw down greater graces on her soul. Call an ignorant person from the world and ask her according to this description which of the two Religious walks in the ways of God, and she will unquestionably make a just decision.

The State of Religious life is sovereign perfection; to live imperfectly therein is unquestionable ruin. Reflect well, my dear Sisters, before you proceed; make every exertion in your power. Efforts must be made for the remaining time to overcome all human and self-love, and having done all you can, let not the remaining embers of your weakness deter you from proceeding. There will be always something to deplore, and there would be neither priest nor nun did they wait till they eradicated all their imperfections. Our perfection does not consist in accomplishing this, but in using diligently every means in our power, and those prescribed for us by obedience, for attaining this end, and in making strong and practical resolutions of avoiding everything that would be in the least displeasing to God, particularly attachment to our own will and judgment, human affections, etc. Human affection does not only consist in being attached to creatures, but also in retaining too strong an attachment to our own opinion on any subject, even in matters apparently good, by acting in opposition to the advice we receive on these occasions from lawful authority.

All human attachments or affections and anxiety about creatures must be now regulated and for the present laid aside, as well as everything else that does not tend to a preparation for this great union with God. By keeping your heart thus fervently united to Him, He will pour on your soul such fervor and consolation as are unknown to the tepid and surpass all the delights of the world, by seeing that you do all in your power to attract His friendship. You should remember that not to advance is to go back, and reflect each day that you can do more to attract God's love and friendship than you did the day before. The best means to obtain this favor is to make frequent acts of the love of God. At first we may not feel this fervor, but it will increase provided we are faithful in the above practice, for the Scripture says, "Love begets love." Those who arrive at this perfect love of God will feel such peace of soul as nothing will be able to disturb.

Section 1: Poverty

As avarice is the mother of all vice, so Poverty is the mother of all virtues, and closely allied to Christ's favorite virtue, humility.[3]

The Vow of Poverty is a second baptism which purifies from all sin. Christ says, speaking of the Religious, I will purify her, not as gold, but in the furnace of poverty. Poverty frees her from all temporal cares and possessions, or a chance of ever possessing them; for although a Religious may not have any property to forsake in leaving the world, yet it does not lessen her merit in the sight of God, for she does not know how far fortune may favor her had she remained in the world, as it has done to many; at least she gives up all hope or desire of possessing, for the poorest in the world may still have the desire of possessing more, but the Religious in making the Vow of Poverty gives up all and has no desire. If she happen to receive the best in food, clothing, or lodging, she is not disturbed, nor does she consider that she violates the Vow of Poverty, as she did not seek these things or desire them; and on the contrary, should she be provided with the worst and most inconvenient, she is equally satisfied and unmoved, as she has given herself entirely to God.

God is pleased that the Religious should rightly understand what she has sacrificed to Him, in order that she may feel more ardor and delight in making the offering of herself and thereby avoid making it in a languishing manner. She should rejoice when she suffers any want or inconvenience, for this is the fire in which Jesus Christ intends to purify her.

The four cardinal virtues are fully accomplished in the Religious who makes this Vow, for what greater prudence than to forsake now voluntarily what she would one day be obliged to leave? As for justice, she is separated forever from having it in her power to defraud others who might be engaged in her service of what they had a right to. She has overcome the world by her fortitude in forsaking it and by breaking every tie that could attach her to it. The virtue of temperance she cannot violate if she observe her engagements, as her time for eating, speaking, sleeping, recreating, etc., are all marked out for her.

"Blessed are the poor in spirit for theirs is the kingdom of Heaven." This poverty of spirit is what would be called in the world a mean spirit, for example, if a person there meets an affront and does not resent it, they would immediately be termed mean-spirited.

Yet this is the spirit Jesus Christ pronounced "blessed," and which a Religious above all should endeavour to acquire. She should make every effort to bring down her spirit and think so meanly of herself as not to be worthy to raise her voice in her own defence, so that those who observe her would be tempted to say, "She does not appear to be sensible of this humiliation" or whatever it may be; "she seems to be more like one dead." Should she on these occasions feel passions rising within her and that she is obliged to use efforts to restrain them, it shows that her spirit is not entirely subdued, and she does not possess in perfection the spirit of poverty and meekness.

In being thus treated let her humble herself before God and say, "In as much as I am to blame or have been the cause of others giving way to impatience, or displeasing God, I am sorry," and let the expression of her countenance be such as to indicate sorrow for the offence offered to God, and not for the injury done herself. She should then joyfully accept of any humiliation that may arise from it, and unite it to those Christ endured for her sake and in atonement for her many abuses of His graces. This is a sure sign that He is leading her into that road which He Himself trod before her, and which is the only safe road to Heaven.

The decrease of ambition is the augmentation of Divine charity. The ambition here spoken of does not altogether consist in coveting the riches of the world, it may also be nourished in the

Convent. If a Religious, for instance, desires that her work should be approved of or praised, or that a Sister should say how well she did such or such a thing, this is ambition. If, on the contrary, she had reason to suppose she should have been the person selected to render some service to the Community, and she finds herself rejected and made a nobody of, let her gratefully accept the humiliation and thank God for it, instead of raising herself in the estimation of anyone.

The Religious who possesses poverty of spirit should be calm and unmoved in all occurrences and accidents of life, and if she should hear of her nearest and dearest relation being on the point of death, she should listen to the intelligence with all possible composure, without showing any of those worldly, unsubdued feelings which are quite contrary to the spirit of the truly poor Religious, but she may evince the deepest interest in all that concerns their souls, and enquire if everything has been done for them. This is what Religion effects or ought to effect: it breaks down the spirit. Why is it that a poor person thinks so little of having a dead person lying in the same room where they are sitting? It is because the spirit is broken down by want, humiliation, and privation, and consequently is not alive to these things. As long as an attachment remains for the most trivial thing, it will deprive the Religious of this spirit of poverty and disengagement of heart. She will not have renounced all for Jesus Christ, and she cannot expect that His promise will be fulfilled in her, Who has said, "He who leaveth mother, or sisters, or brethern, etc. for My sake shall receive an hundred fold here and in the next life everlasting happiness."

She should consider herself with the Apostle a stranger and a pilgrim on earth, having her conversation in Heaven. This is the happiness of Religious life, as every day she is preparing to enter into her own country, and wishing when she retires to rest for that happy hour, not having anything to attach her to this world. "Seek first the kingdom of God and His justice and all other things shall be given to you over and above."

God's justice requires of a Religious that she be stripped of everything. She must no more take or appear to take any interest in the concerns of her friends; she must be deaf and dumb to all their affairs if possible; otherwise, she is not seeking or fulfilling "God's justice." This seeming indifference to their concerns will give more edification to worldlings and draw down greater graces from God than all the austerities or works of mercy she could perform.

A Sister is not, however, to appear with a methodistical countenance or become a preacher to her visitors by her words; but her happy, cheerful countenance and edifying, innocent behavior should preach to all. In discharging her duty well with visitors, she is seeking and satisfying the justice of God as well as in the faithful discharge of every other duty and precept; also in embracing humiliations and the cross, in whatever shape it shall be offered, for having united herself to a Crucified Spouse, she must endeavour to render herself conformable to Him. Let her remember that her cross must be composed of something, and God Himself wishes to become her inheritance; she should therefore go on with great confidence of arriving at her end, for He will be with her in her affliction. In withdrawing her from the world He does not intend withdrawing her from sufferings; for this would not be consistent with her state of banishment, but He will sweeten them for her, having tasted them first Himself.

Christ said to His Apostles that He would cause them to "sit on twelve thrones." Cherish your happy state of Poverty which promises such great rewards, with a heart overflowing with gratitude to God; for the same promises that He made to His Apostles He makes to Religious who live up to their Vow of Poverty, and they are so great that He cannot bestow greater.[4]

As the most acceptable return a benefactor can receive from those on whom he bestows favors is a countenance testifying the gratitude of the heart, how acceptable must it be to God when we make Him this return, shewing to all by our happy, cheerful countenance the gratitude with which our hearts overflow towards Him, for His many favors in this life and His great promises for the one to come. To whom did He make these great promises? To poor fishermen who had nothing to leave but a boat and nets, showing that He does not regard so much what we leave as the will wherewith we leave it.[5]

We should understand well what Religious Poverty is; it is an entire abnegation of Self and a spirit entirely broken. The Religious should consider herself a mere abject, a nobody, and she proclaimed aloud that she has chosen to be this, so that no matter how she is treated, or by whom she is neglected, she is not to be surprised, or take notice of it, unless the spiritual welfare of the person require it, or the duty she has entrusted to her care render it necessary.

In food and raiment she should always desire to have the worst allotted to herself, in order to imitate Jesus Christ crucified more perfectly,[6] but should even the best be given her, she is not to be uneasy or suppose she has violated the Vow of Poverty. On the contrary, should she obstinately refuse them, she might *then* have some fears of violating it, as she would be usurping to herself the power of making a choice, which she had sacrificed to God. The Religious should resolve that, after she makes before the Bishop, Clergy, Community and people, but above all, before God and His Angels, the public declaration of becoming an abject in His house, she will never act contrary to it.

If when spoken to, in what she considers an unkind, humiliating manner, she should retire and indulge herself crying or lose her time in dwelling on these circumstances, how unlike is she to the abject Religious? When or how does she expect to take up her Cross and follow Christ, if she is not to meet with it in those with whom she associates? When slighted or neglected, she should rather be surprised she does not receive more, and when taken notice of or accommodated she should feel quite confounded at it. Humiliations, abjection, and sufferings are the consequences of Poverty.

Had Jesus Christ gone about as a great one of the earth, followed by a train of attendants, He would never have been treated as He was, but as He chose a state of Poverty, He would also suffer, so a Religious, following the example of Christ, and making choice of Poverty, signifies also her desire of suffering with Him.

The fruits of Poverty are great peace of mind, under all circumstances, so that nothing, not even the death of the most beloved member of the Community, should disturb or alter her happy countenance, because she lives by Faith, refers all to God, and looks on this trial as a means of drawing her closer to Him. The second fruit is great joy in the Holy Ghost. A Religious should examine are these her sentiments. If not, there must still exist, within, some secret attachment; she should see where the fault lies and endeavor to remedy it immediately.

The Vow of Poverty in separating us from creatures does not render us less useful to them; on the contrary, the Religious who gives herself entirely to God, and separates her thoughts from all solicitude about her friends in the world and their concerns, would obtain more from the Almighty in five minutes' prayer than she would in five months were she over-anxious or solicitous about them.

The first Virtue that should accompany Poverty is Humility. Religious should cherish this precious Virtue and be careful never to separate it from Poverty, to which Jesus Christ has so closely united it. What could be more contrary to Humility than to hear a Religious speak in an authoritative tone of voice, to give her opinion in a confident, decided manner, when she should consider her opinion as nothing and herself a nobody?

The second Virtue that accompanies Poverty is Patience. You should now in imagination place yourself in circumstances of actual Poverty, to which in Religion you may be reduced, and which cannot be guarded against, and there excite in yourself a firm resolution to bear whatever privations you may be exposed to, if not with joy at least with patience. We may meet with the same losses that others have experienced and want even the necessaries of life, without any other resources than patience and confidence in God; for we could not, like persons in the world, apply for relief to our friends.

The third Virtue is Labour. This has been imposed by God on our first parents and their posterity. Jesus Christ has given us an example of it in His own person, by laboring at a carpenter's trade for so many years of His mortal life. What makes this Vow of Poverty so acceptable in the sight of God is the necessity under which the Religious is of laboring and performing mean and humiliating offices if Obedience require it. In the world she might have labored from natural inclination, but here she is under the necessity of performing her own duties. She cannot say, I am not inclined to perform such a duty today; I can put it off, or get someone else to do it for me.

These Virtues become exceedingly valuable and meritorious in the sight of God if practised in imitation of Jesus Christ, but if His example is not kept in view in the performing of them, they will have but little merit. For example, if a Religious has an opportunity of practising Meekness and Patience, she should reflect how Christ practised them when dragged through the streets of Jerusalem and in all the other stages of His Passion, and say, "Lord, I shall bear this in imitation of Thee." If she does what depends on her, His grace will not be wanting to her. He knows her weakness, having taken it on Himself, giving her an example how to overcome it.

He has not only done this, but has given Himself to be her food in the Blessed Sacrament. As one Communion would be sufficient to sanctify her soul, if it were made with the necessary dispositions, with what fervor and holy desires should not the Religious prepare herself, believing as she does that her Redeemer is contained under the small particle, and that under the appearance of bread is His Body and Blood, Soul and Divinity as He is in Heaven?

The great graces He bestows in the Blessed Sacrament, He particularly promises to the Voluntary Poor, and the reason He bestows more on them, than on those who are poor from necessity, is that the latter have not engaged themselves to be deprived of any property that might be left to them, nor are they so from choice, although they may be perfectly resigned and content, whereas Religious bind themselves to be deprived of All, no matter how little that "All" may be, and of whatever they may have a chance of possessing.

We never can sufficiently admire the example of Poverty Jesus Christ gives us in the Blessed Sacrament. When preparing His Disciples for their belief in this great mystery, He said, "Unless you eat the flesh of the Son of man and drink His blood you shall not have life in you," for He only considered this life as a passage to the other. The Jews said then, as our adversaries say today, "How can this man give us his flesh to eat?" But Christ did not let them go without endeavoring to convince them that it would certainly be done, though without telling them how, for then there would be no exercise for their faith or submission of understanding on which above all things man prizes himself most. He said to them, "Do my words scandalize you? What will you say when you see the Son of man ascending into Heaven?" As if He would say, Will you be sorry then for not believing? And turning to His Apostles, He said, "Will you also leave me?" but Peter said, "Lord, to whom shall we go? We know that Thou are the Son of God." He did not say he understood how it would be, or that he was more enlightened on the subject than those who departed from Him—no, for he was just as ignorant as they were, but professing Him to be Christ, the Son of God, was sufficient to silence all his doubts, knowing that, "with God all things are possible."

Nothing is more worthy of our admiration than the Poverty and Simplicity our Saviour gives us an example of in the Blessed Eucharist. He leaves no difficulty in the way: the matter being only bread and wine, the poorest country can procure sufficient for the celebration of those Mysteries, and the simplest priest can perform the ceremony. Although the discipline of the Church has been altered and the divine mysteries are performed with more pomp than when our Saviour instituted them (through respect for these great mysteries), yet the matter of this Sacrament has never been altered.

Consider the Poverty of Jesus Christ on the Cross, stripped of His clothes, forsaken by His friends, and even by His Eternal Father. He was silent under His other torments, but when that interior support was taken from Him, He cried out, "My God, My God, why hast Thou forsaken Me?" The Religious soul, considering this great Poverty of her dear Saviour, should resolve to bear patiently, if not joyfully, those interior trials she may meet with, and also all contempt, privations, and indigence to which her state of life and poverty is liable, and unite them to those which her dear Redeemer endured for her, saying, I thank you, my God, for granting me a share in your sufferings. She must renounce all property and desire of possessing, also the power of giving and the honor attached to it. She should, as much as possible, avoid distinguishing herself from the other Sisters in any way, and if she should become remarkable at all, let it be for not being remarkable and for being the most hidden and unknown.

It is said of Our divine Lord that "He was always pleasing to behold." It gives great edification to Seculars to see Religious orderly in their appearance, and they should carefully avoid every thing bordering on negligence or disorder in their persons.

Having considered the Poverty of Jesus Christ, the Religious should next keep in view the Poverty of the Blessed Virgin who is also her model. It is piously believed that the Blessed Virgin in imitation of her Son made a Vow of Poverty, reserving only what was necessary, and that she made this Vow, before she knew she was to be the Mother of God, by divine inspiration, that she might be worthy to become the Mother of Him who was to give such an example of Poverty. Beg of her to obtain for you that precious virtue, and humility, its inseparable companion. She says, "because He has regarded the Humility of His handmaid," for if she had ever so much purity and innocence without Humility, God would not have regarded her.

Section 2: Chastity

The Author of this precious Virtue is God Himself. He brought it from Heaven and came on earth to show us how it ought to be practised. Thank your divine Redeemer for calling you to imitate such an example. Renounce all earthly affections which would place an obstacle to the practice of this Virtue. In vain would you go through the Ceremony of Profession, to little purpose would the Bishop and Priests offer up their prayers for you, if any thing remains in your heart, manner, or conduct that would not be conformable to this Virtue. God grant that you may understand well what the Vow of Chastity contains. It is not merely to lead a single life that you engage yourself. Chastity is like a beautiful mirror which the least breath tarnishes.[7] It is customary to say, in comparing a picture with the original, if there be any defect in it, that "it is not a chaste copy," and though a painting might not appear to have any defect to a passing observer, yet when examined by a good judge many would be discovered. In like manner, if there be any thing trifling in the manners of a Religious or contrary to the original of which she is supposed to be a copy, which is Jesus Christ, she cannot be called chaste. It is a departure from the perfection of Chastity to speak in a loud tone of voice. She should recollect in conversation the measured manner in which her divine Model spoke, using only necessary words. What makes this Vow so pleasing in the sight of God and renders those who make it so pleasing and so dear to Him, is that it makes them more like Jesus Christ.

The constant practice of humility, with detachment from creatures and mortification of the senses and inclinations, is, as Jesus Christ has testified by the example of His life, the best means to obtain and preserve the virtue of Chastity. Beg the Blessed Virgin, St. Joseph, and St. John to obtain that precious gift for you, which they possessed in so eminent a manner. Beg it also of the Angels, of whose life yours is an emblem. Diffidence in yourself, with holy fear and confidence in God, is a great means to preserve this Virtue.[8]

The life of a Religious is in three ways conformable to that of the Angels. First, in employment. Their occupation is to praise and adore God continually, without interruption. The employment of a Religious or one aspiring to perfection should be just the same. No occupation withdraws her mind from God, since all is done for Him and in Him. Being entirely separated from the world, she should never be heard to say she was so distracted, she could not attend to such or such a duty. The Scriptures say, He who withdraws himself from God is lost, not only those who withdraw themselves by sin, but those Religious who allow their thoughts and affections to be occupied with things contrary to their state. Their whole life should be a continual act of praise and prayer, often in the day raising their hearts to God by fervent ejaculations, and begging the grace to spend that day at least in His service.

Beg of the holy Angels, particularly your guardian, to obtain this grace for you.

The second resemblance the life of a Religious bears to that of the Angels is that of their habitation. As Heaven is quite different from any earthly habitation, so a Convent is entirely different from any house in the world. Entirely separated from it, they know not, or at least should not know what passes there, and if, at any time, they have to converse with its inhabitants, they should resemble the Angels who, when appointed by God to assist man in any way, they obey, but in doing so never lose sight of the presence of God. Thus the Religious will converse with Seculars at the command of her Superiors, like the Angels in the presence of God, and to promote *His Glory,* not for any self-gratification or for the love of creatures, which she has entirely renounced.

The third resemblance is in Purity, the Angels having no care but to please God and accomplish His Holy Will. The good Religious keeps herself as much as possible in the same state, nor does she permit her thoughts for one moment to be directed to any other object. Religious should proclaim aloud, both by word and example, that by Vow they belong entirely to God, and possess nothing of the world, disapproving of what He disapproved, and giving the preference to what He preferred.

Another great advantage arising from this Vow is that it unites those who make it more closely to God, and entitles them to the privilege of "following the Lamb whithersoever He goeth." A Religious leaving the world should not only have in view an entire separation from the world, but also a perfect union of herself with God. To accomplish this, two things are necessary, disengagement from creatures, and great purity of soul and body. By this union Jesus Christ shares His gifts with His Spouse, bestowing on her His own virtues. She should not rely on her own strength for doing anything, but depend entirely on Him for assistance, which He will not refuse. She in return gives her will, affections, and entire liberty; if she make any reserve, He will not give her that share in His favours He otherwise would. She must never look back, but prepare with courage for the difficulties which may occur, putting all her confidence in God. He who called her to share His sufferings will not fail to assist her in those trials that will come.

Those who make this Vow put it entirely out of their power ever to act contrary to what it obliges, under pain of eternal damnation, which greatly increases its value. Those who are strict in its observance Christ rewards by bestowing on them the precious gift of lively Faith which makes them shun the smallest occasions that could in the least tarnish the lustre of this delicate virtue. This was the object of all the austerities and mortifications of the ancient Fathers: namely, the preservation of religious Chastity. The Spouse is compared to an enclosed garden where all the virtues flourish. The Religious must withdraw herself from all created objects and live to God alone in solitude, even though she were engaged in the midst of a city in the most distracting occupations. When with visitors, or discharging a duty of this nature, a sister can never say, "This time is at my own disposal. I am not now engaged in any spiritual exercise and need not be so much upon my guard." No, she must never be unmindful of her engagements, or leave her solitude. If she does not guard her heart, by the mortification of her senses, a breach will be made and a crowd of worldly thoughts will rush in and destroy its repose. She should never view any object through mere curiosity; either the glory of God, her own or her neighbour's salvation, must be the motive. She should mortify the sense of hearing by refusing it the gratification of listening to vain, useless, and unprofitable conversation. She must be careful in the observance of silence, following the advice of St. Gregory who says, "Consider if what you are going to say be better than silence; if not, hold your peace."

This continual watchfulness and restraint may appear tiresome and laborious, but consider how short a time it will last, and the eternal reward it will purchase. Even in this life God bestows great favors on those who are thus faithful, changing their solitude into a paradise of delights. But this withdrawing herself from creatures and created objects must be with the Religious interior as well as exterior. It would signify little to withdraw the body and consecrate it to God, wearing the holy Habit of Religion, if the sacrifice of the mind and heart did not accompany it.

Section 3: Obedience

This is the most excellent of the three Vows made by Religious,[9] the other two being but part of the sacrifice; but this includes all the rest, as it is through obedience they are made. Poverty and Chastity can be, and have been, practised by vow in the world, but obedience belongs particularly to Religious. It is the surrender of her own will and judgment to that of another; the voice or command of her superior is to her the voice of God.[10] It would therefore be very dangerous to stop and reason on the command she received, or allow herself to think that those who direct her had not sufficient judgment or experience, and that her own way of acting should have been much better. She is to give up this darling self-will and judgment, and exactly and with simplicity do what is prescribed; and although the person who commands may not possess much judgment and experience, yet when the subject acts through a motive of obedience, she will always find matters turn out better than if she acted according to her own ideas; or there will be some secret good concealed in it, which she cannot discover. She should never act from the conviction that the person who directs her is one of judgment and experience, but because this is what the spirit of religion requires.

It is this Vow that makes the Religious, and therefore is more excellent than the other two because it comprises the whole sacrifice.[11] If a person about to enter a convent were asked, What vows are you going to make? What Rule are you to observe? She would probably answer, "I do not exactly know. I am going to become a Religious, and to do whatever I am told." The Religious should also endeavor to do the will of her equals in order to bring her mind to a state of submission. Beg of God to grant you grace to understand well all that this Vow contains and faithfully to put it in practice. By it you return to God the most precious gift He has bestowed on man, and on which man prides himself most.

To render obedience perfect, the Religious must take care not to act through any human affection she has for the Superior, or dependence on her judgment, but because such is the order God has established for religious life, and because it is His holy Will. If she act thus, and is faithful to the smallest observance, she will obtain the three prerogatives attached to perfect obedience. The first, that by it she substitutes the will of God for the will of man, with greater certainty than if an Angel spoke. The second is that she still more closely unites herself to God by making His will hers. The third, that she gives great glory to God by sacrificing what is most noble in the noblest work of creation.[12]

It is a usual saying in the world that one is never a good judge in their own cause, and prudent persons, if they have anything of consequence to settle, will generally seek advice of some experienced friend to direct them; and the more prudent they are, the more likely they are to act thus. How much more necessary is it to submit to the guidance of another in an affair of such great importance as that of eternal salvation?[13] A Religious may perhaps say she has the gift of understanding, and why not make use of it? She does make the most excellent use of it by submitting it to the will of God in the person of her Superior, whether that Superior be a person of information or not. It has been decided by the Church that the words of our Saviour, "He that hears you hears Me," relate to all Religious Superiors.[14] We may be as certain that what they require of us is the will of God, as if we had it in our power to retire to some particular place, and then hear His own voice directing us, or as if He took us by the hand, and said, "Follow Me," this is the way in which I would have you to walk.

This virtue of obedience purchases for the Religious a liberty and peace beyond all expression; she can with certainty say there is nothing on earth can give her any trouble, for she takes in exchange for her own will that of God. Her superiors being the channel through which His will is conveyed to her, He will never fail to direct and inspire them with what will tend much to the sanctification of the souls under their guidance. A Religious should then always obey with simplicity, and should only exercise her understanding in the discharge of her own particular duties; for then she is to trust that God will give her all that is necessary, believing that it is well for her to be placed in a state in which she is to make no other use of it. God says He will comfort and console the Religious as the loving Mother cherishes her child, which is the greatest example of affection He could give. What a pity not to do everything to deserve the affection and assistance of such a Father by seeking to please Him in everything and submitting with confidence to His holy will, knowing that whatever is required of us is either by His direct appointment or permission, and that nothing can happen without His consent, how trifling soever it may be.

The Vow of Obedience has three degrees of perfection.[15]

(1) The first is to do exactly the thing commanded, even the smallest observance, following in this the example of Jesus Christ Who did not leave unfulfilled the most trifling of the prophecies, showing that as He consented to fill that state He would do so with the utmost perfection.

(2) The second is to obey because it is the will of God, and from that motive to anticipate the will of superiors, by doing not only what they direct to be done, but what you think they would wish you to do. An excellent model of this obedience is a little child who loves its mother, and is brought up in the practice of obedience. When she tells it to do anything, how foolish soever it may be, it would instantly do it, without making any objection, although she may call it afterwards a foolish child for doing so.

Persons who thus give up their will may be said to bury it, and their superior is its tomb;[16] or, as St. Ignatius beautifully expresses it, they are like dead bodies who do not stir without being moved by others.[17] Our Divine Lord has given us an example of the ardent desire we ought to have of doing the will of God, when He said "My meat is to do the will of My Father." It was His very nourishment. Endeavor then to attain this degree, in which consists your happiness and advancement in perfection. It may appear difficult at first, but by practice it will not only become easy but delightful, for Jesus Christ has said "My yoke is sweet and My burden light." He calls it a "yoke" and a "burden," but by His grace it will become easy and less burdensome than a departure from this virtue.

(3) The third is to do what is prescribed without exercising the understanding, and the motive of this obedience should be that God's will is confided to your Superiors, and that it is through them He is pleased to make it known to you. You should then obey and submit your judgment as in matters of faith. Take the Blessed Virgin for your model in this degree of obedience, and in the three virtues which particularly characterized her: humility, resignation to the will of God, and an entire abandonment into His hands.

It will be well to mention here your obligation to obey all in office and to do every thing prescribed by them as you would if it were the Superior herself. They are appointed to the different offices by her, and it is enough for you to know that they are in them by proper authority. In refusing to obey them, you would refuse to conform to the regulations and appointments of the Superior.[18] You should never interfere with the office of another or their employments, which would be the cause of great irregularity and disturbance. Neither should you seek for or refuse an office, but when you are charged with any, try and have a holy love for it because it is God Who has allotted it to you.

Observe your Rules faithfully, as on their exact observance depends your perfection. A great means to effect this is to love them because they are a manifestation of God's holy will, and observe the same exactness in fulfilling them as you would the commands of your Superior and from the same motive.

Pray often for the great grace of perseverance on which depends the reward of all your efforts. Often consider the example Jesus Christ gives you in His sacred Passion. Obedient to His Eternal Father, to Pilate, Herod, and the priests, making no distinction, because He knew that in obeying them He was fulfilling the will of His heavenly Father. He was truly a dead body in their hands, dragged from one place to another without making any resistance or uttering a word of complaint. The martyrs spoke, and were even delighted to have an opportunity of doing so in defence of the cause for which they suffered, but Jesus Christ was silent, from which we may learn the enormity of sin, which caused such suffering in the Son of God.

Consider too the example of obedience Christ gives us in the Adorable Eucharist. He is indifferent as to what part of the world He is offered up in, or what kind of houses, whether a stately church or a poor cabin. How at the voice of a weak man He changes the bread and wine into His own Precious Body and Blood, but not until the moment *that* man utters the awful words. It is not wonderful that the creature should obey the Creator, but it is most wonderful that the Creator obey the creature; yet behold His submission and His indifference in being employed in whatever way man pleases, whether He is offered as a sacrifice of thanksgiving or atonement, to be employed in visiting and comforting the sick, or to lie concealed in the Tabernacle. Learn from this example a perfect obedience and indifference to all employments, and as water assumes the form of whatever vessel it is put into, so do you form your heart and will to love and fulfill whatever shall be assigned you, for the love of Him Who has ordered it so.

The most trifling thing foretold by the prophet of our Divine Saviour He fulfilled, so that He might well have said hanging on the Cross, "It is consummated." See if you can say the same. Do you perform exactly all that is prescribed for you? When desired to do anything in a manner you do not like, and your judgment may dictate what may seem better, or when desired to have such and such a person assisting you, do you make any objection? Or do you follow the example of Jesus Christ Who when He heard the kind of death He was to suffer, and with whom, did not say He was very willing to suffer death, but not in the company of thieves. No, He was silent then, as well as in all the other stages of His Passion. He says, "Father, into Thy Hands I commend My Spirit." Do you the same by the vow of obedience, sacrifice into His hands that spirit of pride, of impatience, self-love, immortification, etc.

Examine how you observe your holy Rules. What is your motive? Is it that you may be thought very regular and an exact observer of them, or to gain the esteem of anyone? Or is it purely for the love of God and that you may be seen and approved by Him alone? How do you conduct yourself towards your Superior? Do you pay her all the respect due to her office and view her in your regard as the representative of Jesus Christ in all she requires of you? Although she may not have much judgment or experience, it should be enough for you to know that she has been duly elected.

Section 4: Charity, etc.

The end of all the preceding instructions should be to attain this great end, the love of God and our neighbor. Consequently this obliges us to promote God's greater glory by our own and our neighbor's salvation.

Humility, meekness, modesty, and a sweet loving conformity to the will of God should be our interior and exterior attendants, not such a conformity as to say, I am content to suffer this affliction, and at the same time to show by our countenance a want of this disposition.

The sister who might have a great deal to do with others, and in giving directions about work and other things, should find them not attended to, must take care then not to act like a mistress in the world. The evils arising from such conduct would be very great. In the first place, she would be departing from what her state strictly obliges her to, which is to give edification by her meekness and forbearance and thus promote the glory of God, her own and her neighbor's salvation, and she may depend upon it that the blessing of God will never attend any of her undertakings which are conducted in a hurried, impetuous manner. She should rather seem to be asking a favor of those she employs, and if they should neglect to follow her directions, she must show by her patience and sweetness that if she feels at all, it is for their having offended God, and not because they have inconvenienced her.[19]

She should act towards them in such a manner that when these young women meet reproofs in the world they may contrast the manner of the mistress, with the humble, gentle manner of the Religious, so that they may be induced to say, "How different is this from what I met in the Convent," and perhaps it may be long after you have departed this life that your edifying conduct to these persons may give glory to God.

This is what would make them esteem and respect you and cause your instructions to have the desired effect; otherwise the whole business would be mere outward show. One word of instruction from the sister who conducts herself in the mild, gentle spirit of her Redeemer will have more effect than all that could be said by another who departed from it.

Your conversation should be always simple and useful. You should observe this gentleness of manner particularly towards your sisters, avoiding all stiffness and reserve, endeavouring thus to draw souls to God. The Religious who acts thus is of far greater consequence and value to the community, though not qualified to fill any office of importance, than she who without these dispositions would be able to conduct the whole business of it.

Our Divine Saviour's example should be before us under all circumstances, particularly in exercising charity towards our neighbour and more especially towards those who are united with us in Religion. See with what affection and meekness He reproves His disciples when He had occasion to do so. Examine if you have a cordial affection for every sister, which consists not in the outward appearance, but in a true, sincere, and heartfelt affection for all, not such or such a one because she happens to be more spiritual, or has more pleasing manners than another. For this would not be loving them as Christ loves us, nor be following the example He has given us, who when Judas approached to betray Him called him by the tender name of friend.

See if you feel coldness or aversion; spiritual writers generally put these two evils together, because if coldness reign in your heart towards anyone, there is great danger of aversion following, and it is usually the result and evil consequence of it. If you find there is a shadow of this vice in your heart, lose no time in rooting it out and endeavour to implant in its place that cordial charity so much recommended. It is by acting thus you will know if you have died that death which the holy Profession is intended to effect and if you have risen to a life of grace.

Another motive which should induce us to be faithful in the practice of this virtue of charity is because it is the command given us by our dear Redeemer at His last Supper. Nothing should make us esteem this virtue so much as the consideration that it was His last and, as we may say, His dying injunction to His Apostles, no less than three times repeated. If the last instruction of a dear friend makes so deep an impression, how much more should not that of our Blessed Saviour, who chose this time to impart this His favorite command as the best calculated to make it be more deeply impressed on the minds of His disciples.

What are the limits He prescribes to His command? He extends it to that which He exercised for us: "Love one another as I have loved you." Our exercises of charity performed abroad will have no value before God if there be not established at home a solid foundation of this virtue, for the Scriptures tell us that, "well-regulated charity begins at home," and it is on these conditions that our exterior duties will be acceptable to Him. If there be anything difficult in this virtue, the example of Christ will make it not only easy but delightful. If a sister appears to receive your attention with coldness and not with that affection you would wish, you should show her by every means in your power that you feel nothing towards her but the most cordial and affectionate charity. A sister who acts otherwise undermines as much as she can the Institute to which she belongs, and is far from obeying the command of Christ, "Love one another."

When God finds a soul unfaithful to Him, and acting with coldness and want of affection, He does not say He cannot act towards her as He formerly did, and that He must withdraw His grace from her, no, but His greatest care is to make her return to Him, and on her sincere repentance remembers no more her sins. How strongly should this example excite all to union and charity if there be any difficulty in the practice, as there certainly may be, when we meet with coldness and reserve for our kindness and affection.

To show the great esteem Christ had for this union and charity, He recommended it three times at His last Supper to His Apostles. He prays five times to His Eternal Father to bestow it on them, saying, "Grant, O My Father, that as You and I are one so these My Disciples may be one with Us." For it is by being united to Jesus Christ that we will be united with each other, and this is the greatest blessing Almighty God can bestow on a Community. God looks on the Convent where perfect charity reigns as a delightful garden, a paradise where He delights to dwell. Endeavour to contribute as far as in you lies to make that in which you dwell such a one in His sight. To effect this you must renounce your humours and evil inclinations, your rights, that is, the desire of being honored and respected, which we may erroneously suppose the dignity of our state entitles us to. For the Religious who desires to give glory to God and to show the real dignity of her state will display it by her condescension and affability to her younger sisters, avoiding all coldness and stiffness in her manner, thus making them ardently desire to be united to Jesus Christ by the holy Profession, which is the greatest happiness she could be instrumental in procuring for them. If she finds herself stiff or cold to any, let her ask herself the question: If every sister found this manner in all, is it possible anyone would persevere in Religion?

Though a Sister's state of health may prevent her from performing any of the active duties of the house, or her incapacity to fill them cause her to think she is of little or no value to the Community, yet if she observe this manner towards all her sisters she is doing a great deal, both for God and the Community; she is then taking an active part in all the duties of the Order. Therefore she should endeavour for the glory of God, the advantage of the

Order, and her own perfection, to bear towards each sister great respect, particularly to those who hold office, by which they are superior to her, though in every other respect they may be her inferiors. For this conduct gives great edification and promotes union very much, for a junior sister seeing a professed act with so much humility and respect, will naturally reflect on her own manner, which otherwise she might never have thought on, and say, How deficient am I in my conduct to others, and yet I see one so much my senior acting as the last of the Community.

The prosperity or advancement of the Order does not depend on, nor is it to be attributed to, the good reader, writer, or transcriber, although these are very desirable, but to the humble, cordial, affectionate, obliging, complying, and charitable Sister.

Zeal for the salvation of souls should be the result of this charity, and how can she show it more than by endeavouring to promote the intimate union of souls with God by the holy Profession. Having laid a solid foundation of zeal and charity at home, she may then with security and fruit exercise it abroad. She should accompany this duty, first, with great charity and tenderness; second, with energy and sweetness; third, with great humility and diffidence in self.

Beg of God earnestly to grant you these dispositions in order that your work may become meritorious and pleasing in His sight. A community in which this universal charity reigns is like a well-arranged army, terrible to devils and capable of surmounting all difficulties.[20] They will continually advance in perfection, and promote not only their own, but also their neighbor's salvation. There may be some difficulty found at first in the practice of it, but we are *bound to it* by *our vows*. It is certainly a labor to be continually fighting against self, but it will soon be over, and the reward will be great. It is not by prayer alone that the Religious of this Institute is to keep herself recollected in God and united to Him; she must endeavor to do so in her most distracting occupations. If this were well observed, how seldom would there be a breach of charity! It is the spirit of charity that will increase the love of God in her soul and render it manifest to all that the love of Him is the motive that influences all she does.

Humility and meekness are the virtues to which you should particularly apply yourself in order to attain this. These are our Divine Saviour's favorite virtues and which He desires us to learn of Him. "Learn of Me for I am meek and humble of Heart."

Mortification is another means most necessary to attain charity and union with God. It consists not so much in practising corporal austerities as in the denial of the will, humors, and evil propensities. Those who complain of nervous and sensitive feelings may depend upon it, it is the want of mortification and a little exertion in overcoming themselves. St. Paul says, "I die daily." The Religious should say the same, and endeavor to make her life conformable to Jesus Christ crucified. Her life should be conformed to all her words and instructions. What are her words? She calls herself a Religious, so she should conduct [herself] in such a manner as would be expected from a Religious.

A frequent reception of the Blessed Sacrament is the most effectual means to obtain this union. It is called holy Communion because it unites many into one. Union and charity are the proper effects of this Sacrament; if these fruits are not produced in the soul of a Religious who so often communicates, she has real cause to be uneasy for no matter what virtue It may seem to have been produced, without this It has not worked Its proper effect in the soul. She should therefore renounce all occasion of coldness or aversion she may feel towards anyone, particularly her Sisters, before she approaches this holy Sacrament.

Having done all in her power, there will be still something to be done, which the weakness of her nature prevents her perfectly accomplishing, but then Jesus Christ comes in this Sacrament to assist and crown her with success. If these holy mysteries were only now instituted, and if we wanted to know who belonged to this new society, we would certainly seek for those who had the marks of union and charity as persons who belonged in a special manner to it, and not for those who spent the most time in visiting the sick, or saying long prayers, though these are very good—when accompanied with the virtue which is the proper effect of this Sacrament, and when they can be practised without prejudice to our Rules and duties.

She should mortify all her passions and humors that Jesus Christ may produce in her soul the effects which belong to this holy Sacrament. Beg the proper dispositions to obtain all the graces annexed to It. He says, "he that eateth My Flesh and drinketh My blood abideth in Me and I in him." If He saw any better means of effecting this union, He would without doubt have had recourse to them and not leave this holy Sacrament exposed to so many insults and abuses which He has so frequently received.

Mortify your self-love—communicate often with this intention. Grace will be given you in each Communion, to overcome all impediments to your perfection, if made with faith and ardent desire of advancing in perfection and virtue. Excite yourself to an ardent love of God and cordial affection for your neighbor, particularly your sisters.

The Religious who perseveres in this constant and unvaried[21] practice of charity, notwithstanding all the coldness she may receive for her services, may be truly said to be preparing others for Communion, and may expect to partake of all the sweetness contained in this holy Sacrament.[22]

A. D. 1832

Editor's Note

The principal *archetype* for the entire chapter 1 is a Bermondsey manuscript whose reference number is IOLM/BER/12/1/4 and which is preserved in AIMGB. Its original composer was presumably Mary Clare (Georgiana) Moore, the founding superior of the Mercy community in Bermondsey (London) in November 1839. Clare entered Baggot in June 1830, was received as a novice on January 23, 1832, professed vows on January 24, 1833, and went to Cork as the founding superior in July 1837.

Derry MS 86, a Bessbrook manuscript titled "The Essential Value for Religious," also corresponds very closely with several parts of this chapter. This manuscript may be attributed to Mary Ann Doyle, who, with Catherine McAuley, professed vows on December 12, 1831, went to Tullamore as the founding superior in April 1836, to Kells in 1844, and then to Derry in 1848, where she died in 1866; or to Mary Teresa Purcell, who entered Baggot Street in early 1834, was received as a novice on July 3, 1834, professed vows in Tullamore on May 27, 1836, became the Tullamore superior in 1844, and died there on March 28, 1853. The vast majority of the Tullamore, Kells, and Derry manuscripts, including Derry MS 86, are now preserved in ASMBNI.

A Liverpool manuscript titled "Mother McAuley's Last Instructions in the Noviceship Baggot Street" and now preserved in AIMGB, also serves as an *archetype* for many sections of chapter 1, including that on chastity. This manuscript—whose reference number is IOLM/LIV/1/1—is probably attributable to Mary Liguori (Frances) Gibson, who entered Baggot Street on May 16, 1841, was received as a novice on August 19, 1841, professed vows on July 12, 1843, and went to Liverpool on August 28, 1843, where she was elected superior on July 17, 1849, to succeed Mary de

Sales White, the founding superior. Mary de Sales entered Baggot Street on June 7, 1836, became a novice on January 25, 1837, professed vows on January 21, 1839, founded Liverpool in August 1843, and then resigned her office on July 12, 1849, due to severe spinal paralysis. She may have drafted or contributed to this Liverpool manuscript. In addition to corresponding closely with parts of chapter 1 of the instructions, the manuscript also begins with a long passage on religious life that is not contained in chapter 1. However, this long passage deals with themes and topics that occur elsewhere in the compilation.

Finally, a Birmingham manuscript titled "Manuscript Meditations copied by Sister M. Juliana [Hardman] in Baggot Street 1840" serves as an *archetype* for parts of chapter 1. Juliana Hardman entered Baggot Street on April 29, 1840, was received as a novice on August 10, 1840, professed vows on August 19, 1841, and went to Birmingham, England as the first superior there on August 20, 1841. Possibly this manuscript, preserved in AUSMGB, with the finding number MS GB 1841/1/400/1/2, is a transcript made by Juliana at Baggot Street of another *archetype.*

The main previously published *sources* for the content of chapter 1 are volumes 1, 2, and 3 of Rodriguez, *The Practice of Christian and Religious Perfection* (Kilkenny: John Reynolds, 1806). Nearly identical passages—in concept if not always in exact wording—frequently occur. These passages correspond with Rodriguez's treatment of humility (2:126–248), fidelity to ordinary actions (1:72–97), and the vows of poverty (3:112–58) and obedience (3:192–263). His treatise on charity (1:136–203) probably also influenced Catherine McAuley's commentary on charity in chapter 1; however, only a few exact correspondences have been discovered, even though chapter 1 of the compilation frequently contains broad summaries of aspects of his treatment of charity.

CHAPTER 2ND

On Imitating Jesus Christ

Look and make it according to the pattern that was shown thee on the Mount. —Exod. 25.40

4th July The sense in which the word "*chaste*" is to be taken as regards a Religious is to be free from all defects, as when we call a piece of architecture "chaste" we mean that there is nothing in it that could offend the eye of the most skilful architect. A chaste Religious will never utter, think, or do anything that Jesus Christ would not have thought, said, or done. No idle or flippant expression will escape her, but a sovereign reserve mixed with cheerful gaiety will be her attendants. She will mortify her senses, her hearing, seeing, and palate, and this not insensibly, but will feel what she sacrifices, and be delighted she has something to offer to her Spouse, to whom she will never fail to present all her little acts of self-denial and by whom the smallest will not be unnoticed *if done* for Him.

The observance of the counsels are [*sic*] necessary to the salvation of a Religious; consequently what would be blameless in a person living in the world would be criminal in a Religious who is specially chosen to be intimately united to Jesus Christ. The most acceptable offering we can make to Him is the sacrifice of our self-will. Whatever is contrary to our self-will must ever be pleasing to God. The more we practise self-denial, the more closely will we be united to Jesus Christ who denied Himself every gratification to testify His love for us, and who expects from us in a special manner a return of love by an imitation of His Life.

5th July To die to self-will is to destroy and put an end to it. This will be extremely difficult as there is nothing to which nature has so great a repugnance, and yet the foundation of religious perfection cannot be laid without it. In order to effect it we must ever bear in mind that in following the will of another we are practising that thing of all others most dear to Jesus Christ. We must not regard the persons in authority, but be firmly convinced they are the channels through which God speaks to us, though our judgment should persuade us to the contrary.

Though another thing may appear better, yet what we are commanded will infallibly be more productive of good, as it and it alone will be attended with the blessing of God. We should also comply promptly, cheerfully, and exactly in time and place; by performing the thing commanded in this manner, we draw down the grace of God, which is withheld, although we perform it but not at the exact time and place commanded. When we consider we will be judged for the graces we have not received through our own fault, it should be a powerful stimulus to excite us to the exact and prompt performance of every duty obedience prescribes.

6th July Renounce the world to follow Jesus Christ! God in calling us to religion has delivered us from dangers to which the best in the world are exposed, viz., a false opinion which reigns in the world with regard to religion in general, a spirit always opposed to the spirit of God, and an anxiety and lawful care inseparable from those living in the world. We also possess three advantages of which the most holy are deprived in the world, viz., we can watch over ourselves without interruption, we enjoy the society of persons whose pursuits are the same as ours and whose example is a continual help to us, we are also delivered from all care and anxiety. The more we consider these advantages, the more we will see the gratitude we owe to God.

Jesus Christ says, renounce the impediment and I will take up my abode with you. In our regard He has removed it from us; as we are withdrawn from the vanities of the world, our rational faculties are improved, and we see in a clear light the nothingness of them. God, in bestowing these advantages on us, designs that we would be more closely united to Him, without division or reserve. To effect this He requires from us a faithful compliance with His inspirations, and a reciprocal love for that which He strongly testifies for us. If we comply with the motions of His grace, He will Himself create this love within us, to accomplish which He has withdrawn us from the crowd. To this paramount object should tend all our meditations, Communions, etc., so that His pure love reigning in us, He may clearly manifest His will in our regard. Labor to accomplish this, and in thus promoting His glory and our own sanctification, we shall deserve, as far as on us depends, to be called and to be in reality His faithful Spouses.

8th July "As little infants you must be born anew till Jesus Christ is formed in you." To have Jesus Christ formed in us is to think as He did, to speak as He spoke, and will as He willed. We must divest ourselves of all opinions, sentiments and judgments, hitherto formed and entertained, which are not conformable to His Spirit. This perfection cannot be attained without difficulty and labor, but to it we are bound to aspire when we enter religious life. This labor must be commenced with sweetness and cheerfulness and persevered in with tranquility and composure of mind, never frightened at the task, but believing that Jesus Christ can and will effect this new birth within us, if we do on our part what He requires. He will point out the way in which He would have us walk without any illusion. He will see the efforts we make to discover His will and will reward them by clearly manifesting it to us, through those He has appointed to be our guides, if we with candor lay our feelings open to them. Yes, if we do this in following those decisions, we cannot err. Sooner would God work a miracle than suffer us to be deceived.

It is not sufficient that Jesus Christ is formed in us; He must be recognized in our conduct, meek and humble as He was, and this not only in the exterior, but chiefly in our hearts. Ever complying, ever forbearing, ever charitable, ever compassionate to the weakness and frailties of others. It is by thus imitating His life that we can testify our gratitude for His signal mercy in selecting us preferably to thousands to be His Spouses. "Let us not love in word nor in tongue, but in deed and in truth."

9th July Renounce yourselves for the love of Jesus Christ. When Jesus Christ calls on us to renounce all for His sake, it is not His intention to leave us friendless or without comfort, but to fill up the vacuum in our hearts with Himself, that is, with delights far surpassing any the world could bestow, and a happiness such as the inhabitants of Heaven alone can enjoy. This is His intention, but we frustrate it if in renouncing the things of the world we make any, even the smallest, reserve. Though it were only a vain desire, or a particular attachment to the smallest thing, this alone would be sufficient to deprive us of the abundant rewards promised even here to those who renounce *all.* In order to keep the Vow of Poverty it is not sufficient to give up the goods and vanities of the world; by it we are also obliged to detach our hearts from all worldly convenience, and to be at all times ready to give up whatever we have the use of. An attachment even to a book would be a departure from the spirit of the vow. The Religious who faithfully observes it will be glad when an opportunity is afforded her of feeling the effects of it by a want of some convenience which she might lawfully ask and obtain.

10th July Imitate the sanctity of Jesus Christ. St. Paul [Peter] addressing the first Christians said to them, "Be ye holy as He who has called you is holy." If such sanctity was required in the general body of Christians, how imperative is it on a Religious to attain it, who should by it be always distinguished from the common faithful. The whole exterior of a Religious should portray this holiness: her gait, her look, her voice. This she can never attain without that interior sanctity, far more valuable than the exterior and of which it is only the emblem and effect. Nevertheless, a Religious who studies the perfection of her state can and will attain both, and will encourage herself by the consideration that this exterior comportment will conduce much to the glory of God. For seculars, when they see the change which religion has wrought, will be much edified and attribute all the merit to its power, and not to us. The thrifty step of a worldling is quite unbecoming in a Religious. In the discharge of her duties it should be quite visible that God alone is her object, and appear as if she had no more life than was necessary to discharge them, so that a secular on seeing her at any moment must at once be struck with the modest dignity of her deportment.

11th July It is a very bad disposition not to attach importance to the commission of the smallest fault, since even the least calls the justice of God to avenge it; and His justice if provoked will far surpass in severity all that the malice of man could invent. Besides, it argues a doubt of His word, for He says, "He that contemneth small things *shall*" (not *may*) "fall by little and little."[1] No one that considers and believes this will expose herself to the danger, for He also says, "Heaven and earth shall pass away but my word shall not pass away." "He that is faithful in that which is least is also faithful in that which is greater."[2] These words should powerfully excite to the faithful performance of the smallest things, for without the grace of God we can do nothing. In these words our Divine Lord, as it were, says: If you do not faithfully perform small things, I will not give you my grace to perform great things. It is a very great illusion of the enemy to make us suppose we would faithfully perform things of importance, if we do not labor to the utmost of our power to acquit ourselves faithfully of the most trifling charge enjoined by obedience. If we do not act thus, we, as it were, call on God not to give grace to us to perform great things.[3]

As self-love is the root of all our faults, to combat it is the most effective means to overcome them. Hence, we must closely watch the intention in performing our actions, the motives that influence them, and when we have attained so far that our hearts tell us God alone is our intention, the performance of His will our motive, we may confidently hope we are gaining ground in the combat.

12th July Jesus Christ became for our example and imitation the outcast of the world, and the last of men. He conversed with sinners, yet He was never sad or troublesome, but of a meek and sweet exterior which beautified His countenance and excited the admiration of all who beheld Him. From this description we are to learn to love being despised. However difficult this is, it is not impossible to human nature; some of the saints have acquired it, and we should continually aspire to it.

We are also to learn ever to carry ourselves with a mild and gentle demeanor, in conversing with sinners, bringing ourselves, as it were, down to them, thereby more effectually to draw them up to God. If our humility springs from the heart, it will never make us sad or troublesome. A religious should endeavor to overcome all the disgusts and repugnances she was accustomed to feel in the world; if not, she makes a reserve in the sacrifice and cannot expect the abundant graces given to those who sacrifice all. If she overcome them, she will never be sad, nothing can annoy her; viewing God in everything she feels indifferent how He may employ her.

A religious may be considered troublesome when she is talkative, remarking, peevish, trifling, making much about nothing, attaching importance to the most trifling things. All this is contrary to the dignity of her state. As her rational powers are enlarged by the exclusion of all vanities from her mind, so it is required from the sister, who in the world might have been considered trifling and little-minded, so far to overcome her nature after entering religion that this appellation could no longer in truth be applied to her, but that her words and entire conduct should ever be guided by reason and evince a well-regulated mind. Her countenance, which is an index of the mind, should be ever sweet, beaming with content and happiness, so that a person beholding it should be so attracted as to desire to behold it again. When a person puts on the king's livery, and degrades it by desertion, death is not considered too great a punishment for the offence. What then must be the crime of a Religious who wearing the livery of the King of kings degrades it by the commission of faults unbecoming the dignity of the state to which she is called (a dignity which cannot be greater), and thus deserting her Lord and King?

13th July Although the perfection of charity is the ultimate end of every religious institute, yet each one is guided by a particular spirit to the attainment of that object. Hence arises the great variety of observances prescribed to each, and it is not only hurtful to neglect them, but Religious ought even to [cherish] an attachment to those observances that belong to the Institute of which they are members, for although we love all Religious, yet we are naturally more closely attached to those living in the same Institute with us. All the Fathers of the Church agree in thinking this the general order of Providence.

If our vocation to Religious life is duly proved, this is not our own work but God's, who could cause the Institute to be formed and to exist without our being created; but having created us, He calls us by a signal mercy to form one of His own immediate family in it. Let us not therefore suppose, however virtuous, talented, or useful we may be in the community, that our loss would be felt even for a moment. After we are gone, everything will go on, no duty will be omitted, just as if we had never existed. As a nobleman could carry on his establishment though all in his service should abandon him, he could with great ease fill their places and perhaps with much more valuable subjects.[4]

A religious who is punctual to regular observance may be called perfect. This regularity attracts the eye of God and draws His special blessing on her. In it consists all the beauty of a Religious house, and the entire life of a Religious. She who observes it will never break her Rule; while on the contrary, she who observes it not, whatever virtues she may possess, can never edify, and with regard to her the greatest stretch of charity would be to let her pass unnoticed. Whilst wanting in *this,* nothing in her, however admirable, could be praiseworthy. Any practice of devotion that could cause a Religious to be absent from the common exercises (except obedience enjoins) will invariably prove to have emanated from the enemy.

Every religious house is an enclosed garden where all virtues are to grow and flourish. It is a school where daily lessons are taught and learned. As a flower in this garden I must sow the seeds of every virtue in my heart, and not be discouraged by its barrenness from persevering in my efforts to make them flourish. For God, to whom nothing is impossible, will, if I persevere, crown my efforts with success. As a pupil in this school it is my duty to learn, and teach by my example every day, useful lessons in the science of salvation and perfection.

14th July To form good resolutions without practising them is to resemble a tree that blossoms plentifully, but produces no fruit, which, however delightful it may appear, cannot be pleasing to the eye of its master who intends it should be productive.[5] It is much safer and much more edifying to practise virtue, than to admire it by words which, however elegant and attractive, will never make so deep an impression on the mind. We should never desire to take a leading part even in virtue. This would be to let a worldly spirit or a love of distinction and preference reign in religion. But as some must take a more leading part in the affairs of the house, such should be firmly persuaded that any in the house could equally well, and perhaps better, fill the same office if obedience enjoined them, and consider them in a much safer and happier condition. We never should speak of our imperfections, no more than of our virtues, but if we really think ourselves as bad as we would be inclined to say, we should feel ashamed of them and labor to correct them.

We are from nature so prone to earth, if we do not continually draw our hearts from visible objects self-love will gain ground and triumph over us. We must unceasingly endeavour to destroy self-will or self-judgment that ever inclines us to think our way, our plans, our opinions preferable to those of others. We can never attain perfection until this is destroyed. The most effectual means to accomplish it is by practising acts contrary thereto, by doing that at which we recoil, by refraining from that which we are anxious to do or feel a pleasure in performing, except it be a duty of obligation. To neglect a duty, however pleasing, from the above motive would be erroneous. Without doing this, abundant opportunities will present themselves, and the more frequently we embrace them, the easier, we may be assured, will we find it to destroy this deep-seated evil of self-will.

It is quite contrary to the state of a Religious to content herself with any less degree of virtue than that which the greatest saints have acquired. It is not rational to suppose we cannot arrive at this. We hope to enjoy the same glory they are in possession of. We have the same means they used. God's power is not limited to time, place, or persons. He can effect in us what He did in them. In fine, to arrive at their sanctity requires no more than simply to perform our daily actions perseveringly and regularly. This is what constitutes the saint. This is the difference between the perfect and the imperfect Religious. One performs her daily actions but not at all times with the same exactness, deferring from time to time her different occupations. The other perseveres at all times in the faithful observance of her daily duties, and pays the strictest attention to time and place in the performance of the most trifling, and thus gains for herself a new grace which God never fails to impart in reward of her fidelity.

If we read of extraordinary things, miracles, etc., being performed by some of the saints, God permitted this not as a testimony of their sanctity, but for the conversion of those who were witnesses of them. The performance of great and extraordinary things is no mark whatever of perfection. There are more saints in Heaven that never did anything extraordinary, and who have perhaps attained a far greater degree of glory than those whose lives were remarkable for great actions. It is not the action but the spirit that actuates it to which God looks and according to which He will judge and reward us.[6]

15th July "All the glory of the King's daughter is from within." Though the life of Jesus Christ was eminent in all virtues, yet poverty, obedience, patience, and humility were those for which He was most remarkable; in like manner to the practise of those virtues should a Religious particularly aspire. Though we can never hope to practise them in the same perfection that He did, yet we should never let it escape from our minds that if we do not endeavour every day to resemble Him more and more, we can never expect to enjoy His company for eternity.

His words are decisive, "Look, and make according to the pattern," and though we may not at all times have opportunities of practising these virtues, we should, by bringing them before our minds, and representing them in as lively a manner as if we were called on to practise them, never cease till we find within ourselves a cheerful willingness to embrace them when they do offer. This [is] all God requires of us.

It is of the first and greatest importance [that] the time of noviceship should be spent in the strictest observance of every duty, and in vigorous efforts to overcome our defects. By it the rest of our lives may be judged, for though it is not impossible to become a fervent Religious after being a tepid Novice, it is extremely improbable. It is not rational to think otherwise, for if during our first fervor and while we have no duty to draw away our minds from attending to our perfection, we do not improve, how can we suppose we will do so when our minds are not so disengaged from business, and when by habit we are familiar with all the means of improvement within our reach, viz., lectures, prayers, meditations, admonitions, etc. If we practise these means without drawing that profit they are intended and calculated to convey, it is irrational to suppose we will do it afterwards.

Moreover and above all, let us remember the term of noviceship is the time appointed by the Church and by God for the rooting out of all vice from our hearts. To effect this, great graces are required, which God will bestow during this time, but if then neglected, who can expect, or who would dare promise themselves those succours at a future period when the time allotted for them is gone by. In fine, a novice who desires to be a good Religious will not let one duty pass over without performing it with such fervor as to draw from it the grace annexed to it. There is no duty to which grace is not annexed, but this grace is given only when the duty is discharged with fervor and exactness.

16th July A novice in forsaking the world should also forsake the things connected with it, that is, its news, its manners, its customs, and though she should be affectionately glad to see her friends and show by her manner that religion has not cooled her feelings towards them, she should even be most guarded in her intercourse with them, never testifying the smallest anxiety to know what is going on in the world, but if they enter on those subjects, show by [her] indifference about hearing them that such things no longer interest her.

When we enter Religion, we make an entire offering of the remainder of our lives to God, our will, our humours, our inclinations. This offering is in itself so pleasing to God that it matters not at how advanced a period of life it is made. He will reward the oblation with the most abundant succours of His grace, provided it is a generous, cheerful, and unreserved one. An inclination to indulge even the smallest imperfection would tarnish its beauty in the eyes of God, and take from it all its lustre.

The change of habit is a new birth, and the term of noviceship a state of spiritual infancy during which, no matter what judgment or experience we may have, we are, and must be assured we are, but infants in spirituality, and ought therefore conduct ourselves as little children, suffering ourselves to be led wherever we are guided, indifferent as to what hand conducts us, or whither we are going, convinced that God will not allow us to be led astray.

We should hunger after spiritual food with as much ardor as infants do after corporal nourishment, and ask, and press for it, with equal earnestness. We should not only have no desire to be preferred or esteemed, but dread and avoid, with diligence, hearing the least word tending to our own praise, how much soever we may despise it. For as it is natural to us to be pleased and attracted with it, and as we always carry this nature about us, the surest and safest way to avoid vain glory is never to give ear to what is said in our praise.

The first and most essential virtue to acquire is humility. Begin with this and you begin well, and a good beginning is generally attended by a good end.[7] This humility must not consist in words, nor even in the cheerful discharge of humiliating offices, for a great deal of pride might be concealed under this mask. It must emanate from the heart and arise from a deep conviction of our own nothingness and dependence on God, well knowing that if He withdraw His supporting hand we will immediately fall. Be assured that the constant remembrance of this truth is the most effectual means to advance in humility.

17th, 18th, 19th July The life of Jesus Christ on which we are to model ourselves was a life of continual self-denial and sufferings. The lively animated spirit by which He was actuated caused Him never to be cast down, but enabled Him to triumph over all difficulties. His sufferings never caused Him to be sad or gloomy. His countenance was at all times delightful to behold, and He was ever pleasing to speak to, even ready under the sharpest pains to administer to the afflicted. Thus should we endeavor to comport ourselves under any trial we should have to endure.

In order to be actuated by the spirit of Jesus Christ, we must study the virtues He practised and make ourselves familiar with them. His meekness ever the same under all circumstances, no less meek amidst the infuriated rabble who sought His life, than when quietly conversing with and instructing His Apostles. His charity ever seeking some plea, if not to extenuate the crime, at least to palliate the offence; cautious of letting a word drop from Him to the prejudice of another, unless to prevent scandal, and even then with the greatest compassion and moderation. No less did this charity manifest itself by works: comforting the afflicted, healing the sick, showing the greatest tenderness for them, and evincing as much anxiety for their relief as if His own happiness depended on theirs. His patience under the severest pains of body and mind. We do not hear of one sentence He uttered expressive of fatigue, weakness, illness, etc., although we know, and should believe, that He subjected His nature to the same infirmities to which we are subject, and had the same difficulties to combat in the performance of His mission which we now have to contend against. His sincerity and love of truth, which commanded the admiration of His most inveterate enemies. In like manner did He practise all the virtues; and this not for any short space of time, but at all times and in the most uniform and undeviating way.[8]

To this we must aspire, taking one virtue at a time, and laboring to practise it to the best of our power. This will be doing as He did, for when we read that we are to be perfect, we can never hope to attain the same degree of perfection. All that He requires of us is to aspire to it to the utmost of our power.

The life and maxims of Jesus Christ should be as a book always open before us, in which we are to learn all that is necessary to know; as a glass in which we will clearly see our defects; and as a seal whose image we are to impress on our hearts.[9]

20th July If we do not form our minds on the maxims of Jesus Christ, we will never acquire His evangelic spirit, but the spirit of the world will reign in us under the religious habit. Our duties will appear inconsiderable, poverty will be disagreeable, and obedience will not be cherished. We should be particularly guarded against a peevish and anxious spirit which is quite opposed to that of Jesus Christ who, as the Apostle St. Paul declares, came to diffuse a heavenly and tranquil spirit, and wishes us even here to live as citizens of heaven. Therefore, all anxious solicitude about past, present, or to come, must be totally banished from the mind, even concerning the advancement of souls committed to our care. Such should be our composure of mind under all events, that the entire failure of our most holy undertakings should not for a moment disturb it.

We should never occupy our minds with such thoughts as, Perhaps I did not say or do as much as I might or ought on such or such an occasion. These thoughts never come from God, and if indulged would lead to insanity, but if when examining our conscience, we discover palpable neglect, let us act as little children, be very sorry and promise never to do so any more. Let this sentiment emanate from the heart, be not peevish or uneasy, no matter how numerous our defects may be. Let us resolve to struggle quietly against them in future, and be convinced that our weakness is such that we will always have something to deplore. This conviction should keep us humble, but ever sweet and calm. This method will be very pleasing to God who knows our weakness and compassionates it. The soul that is truly conformed to the will of God will very quickly attain this serenity of mind. Let circumstances most calculated to disturb her take place, she reflects for a moment that they have happened as all things must, by God's will or permission, and her peace is secure.

21st July A Religious should be the child of prayer. The best preparation is constant recollection; let the mind be frequently occupied with pious thoughts, and meditation will flow upon it. To every prayer there are graces annexed which are lost to us if we do not make it with proper dispositions; that is, if during the time of prayer we indulge any thought, however innocent, that does not tend to our spiritual improvement. On the contrary, if we were only to say an "Our Father," if it be said from the heart, an additional grace is given, and though very often that grace is not manifest to us it is nevertheless certain.

God has established as a law that His graces should flow to us through the channels of prayer and the Sacraments; and they are so united that the performance of one is a preparation for the other. Prayer is a plant the seed of which is sown in the heart of every Christian, but on the care we take to nourish and cultivate it entirely depends its growth; if neglected, it will die; if nourished by constant practice, it will blossom and produce fruit in abundance.

Live by the Holy Communion! A Religious should esteem it her greatest happiness to be united to her Spouse by Holy Communion. She has left the world to be more intimately united to Jesus Christ; it is by frequent Communion she will attain this union. On frequent Communion she should depend for the continual help she stands in need of, to persevere in the way she has begun, and should therefore be careful to avoid whatever might be a real obstacle to Its reception, and be cautious of abstaining without just reasons; nay, to abstain without just cause betrays a want of love, gratitude, and fidelity. For if we loved doubtless we would wish to be intimately united to the object of our love. If grateful, we would testify it by acts most pleasing to our benefactor, and we cannot do anything more pleasing to Him than to feed frequently on His adorable Body. If faithful to all our duties, etc., we will never be deterred from Holy Communion by our imperfections or faults; on the contrary, as long as they are not deliberate, we should be the more anxious to Communicate, that we may thereby obtain strength to overcome them.

Jesus Christ did not say, Come to Me you that are free from faults, but "Come to Me all you that labor and are heavy laden and I will refresh you." In fine, to effect this union was the end of His Life and Passion. Knowing our weakness as He did, the greatness of His love caused Him to leave us this sovereign remedy. All His previous miracles were, as it were, preparative to this greatest of all miracles. When numbers of His disciples forsook Him rather than believe this miracle of incomprehensible Love, He turned to His Apostles and said, "Will you also leave Me?" as if He would say, Except you firmly believe that My Flesh *indeed* and My Blood *indeed* is contained in this Sacrament, you cannot be My disciples. I say It is contained in it. Should not this be sufficient for you? Cannot I who have performed so many miracles before your eyes perform this one also? "Except you eat the Flesh of the Son of man and drink His Blood you cannot have life in you." Moreover, every Host that is consecrated manifests the power of God, and consequently promotes His glory, so that by abstaining from Holy Communion without lawful impediment at the appointed time, we rob God of a part of the glory due to Him. This sole reflection should be sufficient to deter us from abstaining.

The best test of our love for God is fidelity to His law. He has said, "If you love Me, keep My Commandments." His law is measured differently to each one according to His calling. Hence Religious, to observe the measure marked out for them, should not only observe the commandments but also the counsels and their Rules, and as the reward, if faithful, is very much greater than that given to seculars, so also their sanctity must far exceed that of the most holy living in the world. No wilful imperfection is admissible in *them*. To attain the love of God, frequent acts of it should be exercised, and if we make this object the end of all our actions, representing to ourselves Jesus Christ in every person we instruct, relieve, comfort, assist, direct, or converse with, if these words of Jesus Christ were deeply impressed on our minds—"Whatsoever you do to the least of these My brethern, you do it to Me"—oh! what a powerful motive would it not be for us to do all our duties in a perfect manner.

Let us be faithful in the exact discharge of our duties. In doing so, we will often have to use violence to our corrupt nature (ever rebellious to restraint), but God will reward us, by bestowing on us the precious gift of holy love; for fidelity is a key that unlocks the treasury of divine love. As persons living in different parts of a kingdom and wishing to arrive at the capital, take different roads, each one taking that which he thinks will lead him there soonest, knowing if he strays out of it he is in danger of not arriving at his destination. In like manner, a Religious, in embracing that Institute which she thinks will lead her soonest to Heaven, should look on the rules and practices as the road marked out for her, and be convinced that she is in danger of not arriving safe at her destined end if she stray from it.

Six defects[10] to be avoided in receiving the visits of secular persons: 1st Prolonging the visit beyond the time which the visitor renders unavoidable, by introducing any new subject or enlarging on the present one, etc., not catching the first moment that civility admits of to stand up, and all coldness of manner, except when intrusive visits may render it necessary.

2nd Appearing too much interested in any family detail. Asking questions that cannot proceed from any useful motive, laughing much, or attending with any degree of earnestness to public and political news.

3rd Neglecting to turn the conversation on some pious matter, and not endeavoring to show by voice and countenance that such discourse only can create a lively interest.

4th To be influenced by any human respect, to seem amused at jests relating to priests or religious ceremonies. To hearken with seeming pleasure or even respectful attention to sarcasms and criticisms on preachers or confessors. To seem amused at any mention of what passed at confession, the penance given, etc.

5th To speak on any interior affairs of the Convent, expenses, recreations, spiritual lectures, tempers and manners of the sisters —though these may seem good, no such conversations should be held on these matters.

6th All frivolous unmeaning laughter, ill-suited to the character of a Religious. High-toned voices or fashionable gestures—all old sayings or applicable phrases. In short, all unnecessary words, gestures, laughter. The whole deportment should be dignified, sweet, condescending—cautiously charitable, avoiding the shadow of a remark not kind or unfeeling, and taking care should any such be introduced to decline it sweetly, mildly, but decidedly, hoping it was not so, and sure it was not intended, etc., etc.

August 1st St. Bernard[11] says the most effectual way to banish gloom and sadness is to live as we ought, to study our obligations, and to fulfill them faithfully. This will seem to us the joy of a good conscience, which is likened in Scripture to a continual feast. This spiritual joy is truly the testimony of a good conscience. St. Francis of Sales [of Assisi][12] says it is one of the fruits of the Holy Ghost. In vain we try to assume it if the heart is not purified and full of humble hope, and if it is, any gloom that may arise will be as easily dispersed as the sun disperses a cloud, or as a spark is extinguished when thrown into a lake. We may be sometimes sad, and divines say there are lawful causes of sadness, as the daily crimes by which God is outraged, our past neglect of His graces, etc. This sadness should be serene, unaccompanied by gloom, taking Jesus for our example, of whom it is said, He was often seen to weep, but never to laugh, and yet the Scripture says His countenance was at *all times* pleasing to behold.[13]

Editor's Note

Four principal *archetypes* underlie most of the wording and content of chapter 2 of Catherine McAuley's instructions: (1) Catherine's own untitled hand-printed manuscript on such topics as recollection, the life and maxims of Jesus Christ, the evangelic spirit, zeal, and Holy Communion. This manuscript, numbered CMA/1/5/2, is in a leather-bound copybook with other manuscripts by other hands, and is preserved in MCA. (2) Catherine's handwritten, selective, and often paraphrased transcription of parts of the first three treatises in volume 1 of Rodriguez, *Practice of Christian and Religious Perfection.* Catherine is said to have made this transcription, now preserved in MCA and numbered CMA /1/5/1,while she was a novice in the Presentation Convent, Dublin. (3) The Newfoundland Manuscript titled

"For Retreat before Reception" and now preserved in ASMSJN. Evidently this record of some of Catherine McAuley's instructions was recorded or transcribed by Mary Francis (Marianne) Creedon, the founder of the Newfoundland congregation, while she was at Baggot Street, Dublin. She entered there on July 4, 1839, was received as a novice on February 27, 1840, professed her vows on August 19, 1841, and departed for Newfoundland on May 2, 1842. (4) The Birmingham manuscript numbered MS GB 1841/1/400/1/2, which is titled "Manuscript Meditations Copied by Sister M. Juliana [Hardman] in Baggot Street 1840." See Editor's Note to chapter 1.

Other *archetypes* for some portions of chapter 2 are a Naas manuscript that is preserved in Naas Box C9 in MCA; and, for one section of the chapter, Birmingham MS GB 1858/10/100/4/1, which is preserved in AUSMGB. This particular untitled Birmingham manuscript (three pages) was clearly handwritten by Catherine McAuley; it contains all the quotations on joy and sadness presented in or underlying the closing passage of chapter 2, under the date "August 1." The analysis given there and the quotations are obviously based on the last pages of Rodriguez's treatise on joy and sadness (*Practice,* 2:333–38).

The Naas Manuscript, titled "Retreat before Reception" and numbered C9/4/4, presumably came from Carlow, from which Naas was founded by Mary Frances Warde on September 24, 1839, and it may have originally come from Baggot Street. Frances Warde was the founding superior of Carlow in 1837. She entered Baggot Street in 1829, was received as a novice on January 23, 1832, and professed her vows on January 24, 1833. Like Mary Ann Doyle and Mary Clare Moore, Frances would have been very knowledgeable about Catherine McAuley's oral instructions in the early 1830s, and may have been the original composer or transcriber of this Naas account of those instructions as well as of the Naas manuscript titled "Instructions before Profession," numbered C9/4/5, and preserved in CMA (see Editor's Note to chapter 4).

The previously published *sources* for the content and wording in chapter 2 of Catherine McAuley's instructions are difficult to establish. Except for a few passages here and there, one has the impression that Catherine's thought in this chapter, while it was certainly influenced by certain books she read, was not dependent on their wording, or else the transcribers simply could not capture in detail what she said. The instructions in this chapter seem to be addressed to women before or immediately after their reception as novices, rather than to those anticipating profession of vows, hence the less systematic and less thorough treatment of the religious vows than, for example, in chapters 1 and 4. Among the *sources* that clearly influenced the content and wording of particular passages are Rodriguez, *Practice of Christian and Religious Perfection,* vols. 1 and 2; Marin, *The Perfect Religious,* of which many earlier English translations from the French appeared from 1762 on; and, in a few spots, Bourdaloue, *Spiritual Retreat for Religious Persons.* Manuscript transcriptions of much of Marin's *Perfect Religious* exist in the Naas and Baggot Street collections preserved in MCA. Illustrative references to these *sources,* where they occur in chapter 2, are noted.

CHAPTER 3RD

On the same Subject, 1834

Learn of Me because I am Meek and Humble of Heart and you shall find rest to your souls. —Matt. Chap. 11, Verse 29

We are all called on to imitate the sanctity of Jesus Christ, and this sanctity should be manifested in our very look, tone of voice, and whole exterior, but this exterior appearance should only be the effect of the interior sanctity we possess, which is far more valuable in the sight of God. Yet this exterior sanctity is also pleasing in the sight of God and gives great glory to His name, for seculars seeing this change which can and ought to be made in a Religious when she leaves the world attribute all to Religion, not to any merit of hers. A clergyman speaking on this subject said he "hated to see a Religious going through her duties with the thrifty step of a worldling and that she should not appear to have more life in her than was necessary for the discharge of her duties, and that if he heard of a Religious in whom this change was not visible he would consider she had not a real vocation."

11th July It is a very bad disposition in the soul to make a great distinction between mortal and venial sin, for Christ says "He that contemneth small things shall fall by little and little." He does not say *may* fall but "shall fall." Christ's words cannot fail.

Self-love is the cause of all our faults, [and] this vice has so many ways of showing itself. If a Religious were desired to do anything, she should never excuse herself acknowledging her inability or want of capacity, but generously undertake it. Should it succeed well and she receive approbation for it, let her offer all to God without Whom she can do nothing. A Religious should never be deterred in performing any work she may happen to be engaged in as well as she can, because the sister who had the same duty before her did not or could not do it well. She is to reflect it is God who employs her, and He will demand a strict account of all His grace enabled or would have enabled her to do had she been faithful.

12th July Jesus Christ became for our example and our instruction the outcast of the world and the last of men. In saying this of Himself by the mouth of St. Paul, He does not intend we should follow Him according to the letter, for this, as well as His other sayings and acts, have a special meaning, but He wished us to learn from this to love to be despised. It is much easier to wish to be unknown than to desire to be known and despised. However, it is not impossible to human nature to have this desire or to put it in practice, though it may appear very difficult. For some saints have acquired this degree of humility. We have the same God to assist us that they had. We should therefore embrace every opportunity He sends us of acquiring it. Jesus was never sad or troublesome, but ever meek and composed in His exterior, which beautified His divine countenance and excited the admiration of all who beheld it. In this too, we should endeavor to imitate Him, for the exterior generally leads us to suppose what the interior is. But these virtues must not merely be put on for a while; they must spring from the heart.

A Religious who is well grounded in humility will never be sad or troublesome, but will endeavor to overcome all the disgusts and repugnances she felt in the world; if not, she makes a reserve in her sacrifice and cannot expect the abundant graces given to those souls who sacrifice all for God. By this victory over herself she will never be sad, for all employments will be alike to her, viewing God's will in each, for the accomplishment of which she entered Religion.

A Religious may be considered troublesome when she is talkative, remarking, peevish, trifling, making much about nothing, attaching importance to the most trifling things. All this is contrary to the dignity of her holy state; and as her rational powers are employed in the service of God and her neighbor, to the exclusion of all vanities, so it is required from the person who in the world might have been considered trifling and little-minded so far to overcome her nature after her entrance into Religion that this could no longer in truth be said of her, but that her words and entire conduct are guided by reason, and show a well-regulated mind. One that wears the king's livery and degrades it by deserting him is not considered to be too severely punished by death. What then must be the crime of a Religious who, wearing the livery of the King of kings, degrades it by committing faults unbecoming her dignity and thus deserts her Spouse and King?

15th July[1] Our Saviour intended, by the answer He made to him who said he would follow Him whithersoever He would go, to show us that in coming to Religion all inclination to any comfort whatsoever [ought to be renounced]. He says, "The foxes have holes and the birds of the air nests, but the Son of man hath not where to lay His head." Our poverty is certainly very far from His; yet we should try to imitate it, and to do so we should bring to mind occasions and circumstances, which perhaps may never occur, of practicing the greatest want. By doing this continually, we come to excite in our minds a desire to suffer this want and so more closely resemble Him. Thus we may be said to practise true poverty by holding ourselves always in readiness for it when it comes.

Although Jesus Christ has given us many examples of different virtues, there are some, such as humility, obedience, patience, and poverty, of which He appears to have given us a more conspicuous example and, of course, which He would wish us particularly to imitate Him in, as they will bring us nearer to Him.

It is of the utmost importance to profit well of the time of the Noviceship, for if we let that time of fervor and greater attraction pass without profit, what will it be when our hearts become hardened and our ears accustomed to spiritual lectures and practices of piety?[2] The time of Noviceship is that appointed by the church for acquiring all the virtues necessary for becoming a perfect Religious and of rooting out of our hearts and overcoming everything contrary to the designs of God over us. God bestows during this time the graces necessary for this purpose, which we cannot expect hereafter if we let the Noviceship pass unprofitably. God bestows graces for the faithful discharge of every duty, which He will multiply according as He sees these duties faithfully attended to, but which He withholds if they are not performed in the place, at the time, and in the manner appointed.

17th July[3] The first virtue which a novice should endeavor to acquire is humility. This humility does not consist in being willing to accept the meanest employments in the house, for there might be a good deal of pride concealed under this disguise, but it consists in having a thorough knowledge of ourselves, as we are in the sight of God, and of our inability to do the smallest thing without His assistance or that of others. This should make us give up altogether making use of the word "I," knowing that if left to ourselves we can do nothing. A sister who cherishes and improves this during the time of her noviceship will lay the foundation of solid piety and perfection and will become the cherished child of God. She should also practice sweetness towards her neighbor, especially her sisters, and docility and submission towards those who direct her, that docility which will convince her that what her Superior desires is really best, although her own judgment may suggest the contrary, for she will consider that it is God who directs all through her Superior.[4]

We cannot become perfect Religious unless we imitate the spirit of Jesus Christ, that spirit of humility, meekness, patience, resignation and sweetness. The Scriptures tell us that "He went about doing good to all," always giving consolation wherever He went, comforting the afflicted when most afflicted Himself, which is quite contrary to worldlings who consider [that] when they are afflicted they cannot comfort others. His was a lively, animated spirit which was never cast down, but triumphed over all afflictions.

Although a Religious should possess talents, accomplishments, and everything that could make her amiable and admired, yet they would be of no value or merit in the sight of God if she possessed not the spirit of Jesus Christ. She should pray most earnestly to Almighty God to bestow that spirit upon her. If she possess His spirit, her salvation is secure. With what earnestness and fervor should she not then pray for it. Let us imitate the Blessed Virgin Mary and St. Joseph whose whole comfort was in the society of Jesus.

18th July Jesus Christ has given us in the Blessed Virgin and St. Joseph an example of what He does for those whom He calls to Religion, by disengaging them from all other enjoyments except those derived from possessing and serving Him. How many are there in the world with a desire of a vocation and have not obtained it? And yet this signal favor is granted us.

A Religious should have recourse to her Divine Saviour in all her troubles and difficulties with a lively faith, which does not merely consist in believing that He knows her wants and can relieve them, but with an enlivening and animating faith which should console and comfort her in the deepest affliction. We should be delighted to make known all our wants and weakness to Him who is willing and able to relieve them, and we should persevere in representing them until we obtain what we want or whatever is His will to grant us.

The life and maxims of Jesus Christ should be for a Religious a book which she should have continually open before her mind, and to take His virtues separately and endeavor to imitate them should be her constant care and study.

19th July In order to imitate Jesus Christ we must often entertain ourselves with Him and study His virtues of meekness, patience, forbearance, obedience, sincerity, charity, and spirit of prayer. His meekness, when suffering the cruelest insults He appeared as little moved to anger, either in words or countenance, as when conversing with His Disciples. His patience, who when suffering the greatest afflictions of mind and body appeared calm and unmoved, nor did He allege any excuse, [such] as want of strength or nervousness. Nor are we to think His being God prevented Him feeling these sufferings as we do, or enabled Him to bear them better. No, we must remember that He took upon Him our infirmities to teach us by His example how we are to conduct ourselves while under similar sufferings, and to endure them with resignation to the will of God. His forbearance, who when listening to language the most calculated to excite indignation forbore making a reply. His obedience to His Blessed Mother and St. Joseph, placing Himself as one under the strictest subjection. His sincerity, which was manifest even to His enemies that all He said must be true, yet it was prudent, reserving all that was not necessary or should not be disclosed. His charity, which showed itself in every way. When accused persons were brought before Him, He endeavored, if not to excuse, at least to lessen their guilt. When the multitude followed Him, although there was nothing He had so much at heart as their eternal salvation, yet He began to feel for their corporal necessities, and said to His Apostles, "I have compassion on the multitude because they continue with Me now three days and have not what to eat, and I will not send them away fasting, lest they faint in the way." It was not from a natural feeling He spoke thus, but to give us an example how to imitate Him. His spirit of prayer. Always before He undertook anything, He prepared Himself for it by prayer, and by prayer He also concluded.

Let us take each of these virtues separately and meditate on the manner in which He practised them, and not leave off until we have succeeded in imitating Him as well as we can in each. Jesus Christ does not intend we should be as perfect as He, when He says, "Be ye perfect as also your heavenly Father is perfect." In order to follow this advice of our Saviour we should endeavor to do each action as perfectly as possible. By doing this we shall be perfect as our heavenly Father. It is only by imitating the virtues of our Divine Master that His designs in our regard can be fulfilled. Let us then beg of Him to prepare our hearts by His lively spirit to receive the impressions of His grace, that His virtues may become fixed therein.[5]

To arrive at evangelical perfection, we must endeavor to imbibe the spirit and maxims of the Gospel. These are to have a high esteem of virtues and sufferings, [and] to consider the contempt in which our Saviour held all earthly distinctions. He says, "Sooner will a camel pass through the eye of a needle, than a rich man enter the kingdom of Heaven"; and again, "By many tribulations you shall enter the kingdom of Heaven."[6] He does not say *may* but *shall,* to let us see that sufferings are the direct path to glory. We see it is not the greatest sinners who are most afflicted in this life, but the most holy.

20th July If we do not conform our lives to the maxims of the Gospel, we can never attain to evangelical perfection, and thus under the Religious habit retain a worldly spirit. Then our duties become unimportant in our eyes, poverty painful, our charity manifests a want of force or life, which Religion gives to those who have its spirit, and which makes us even on earth live as citizens of heaven.

Be not over anxious about anything, even what is good in itself, as our duties or care of souls. We should endeavor peaceably to discharge those duties as well as we can, and if we fail in any of them, let us confidently ask pardon of God, but without any fretful anxiety, which would be very displeasing to Him. He says, unless you become as little children, you will have no share with Me. We should then imitate the simplicity and sincerity of little children, who when they have committed a fault ask their parents to forgive them and promise not to commit it any more, and they are perfectly sincere in what they say.

Jesus Christ came to infuse a heavenly tranquil spirit, and we should particularly guard against anything contrary to this spirit, such as looking too scrupulously into our words or actions, imagining if we had spoken with more zeal on such or such an occasion, or not spoken so much, we would have contributed more to the edification and salvation of our neighbor. If on examining ourselves we find we have acted wrong, we must not on any account become disturbed, or peevish, but calmly imitate the child—express sorrow for the fault, and promise amendment for the future. We should be convinced of our weakness and that we shall always have something to deplore, which should very much conduce to make us humble. We should under all circumstances resign ourselves to the will of God, by whose permission these things happen.

Fervent prayer should be the life and soul of a Religious. She is the daughter of prayer, and should implore her Heavenly Father to bestow this spirit on her. In going to prayer, it is not sufficient to make a general resolution of praying without distractions, but we must propose to ourselves some practical means in order to keep our attention fixed. For instance, in saying the "Hail Mary," to imagine we are looking at the Blessed Virgin while we repeat it, and that we behold her obtaining our requests in saying the "Hail Mary." By this or such other like means as our devotion may suggest, we may come to pray without much distraction.

It is of the greatest importance never to let any instruction, prayer, or psalm pass without endeavoring to draw from it some profit to our soul. We must labor for perfection and to acquire the knowledge of the science of the saints, just as an apprentice would to become perfect in his trade. It is generally by his application while an apprentice that we form an idea of the knowledge he has attained. We may often hear it said, I know what kind of an artist he is, for I knew him [as] an apprentice. The same may be said of a Religious. I know what kind of a nun she is, for I knew her when a novice.

21st and 22nd July The first preparation for prayer is recollection. For this end we must dismiss every thought, no matter how trivial or how good in itself, if it would not be of some profit to our souls. By this means meditation will flow upon us. It is not at the moment of prayer that we are to prepare for it; we must have our hearts ready for it before the time comes. A good method to keep our minds recollected would be to think of heaven and the employment of its inhabitants, or to think of the numbers who are employed throughout the world in the service of God and to compare their happiness with that of worldlings. These or any other profitable thoughts will serve also to entertain the mind. Graces are bestowed on us for the efforts we make in God's service; we should then be ever ready to receive them. Prayer and the sacraments are the channels by which God communicates His graces to us; the well performance of the one is a preparation for the other. Prayer is a plant, the seed of which is sown in the heart of every Christian. If it be well cultivated and nourished it will produce abundant fruit, but if it be neglected 'twill wither and die.

A Religious should consider frequent Communion her greatest happiness, as it is the sweet means of becoming united to her heavenly Spouse here and of securing the eternal possession of Him hereafter. Therefore, she [will] not permit any frivolous occurrences to prevent her approaching the most Holy Sacrament, and she should carefully avoid every real obstacle to Its reception. No trouble of mind should prevent her approaching It except that which proceeds from wilfully consenting to what is sinful. She should prefer saying "*I must go to Holy Communion* because my mind is disturbed," rather than "I must abstain from It on the same account." Jesus Christ says, "Come to Me, all you who labor and are heavy laden, and I will refresh you." He does not say whether it be with sin, sadness, distractions, or *what,* but that He would refresh them. It was to accomplish *this* that Christ suffered all He did; it was for *this* He was born in a manger, labored, and performed so many miracles, for it was not necessary He should have done all this to redeem us. The act of His Incarnation was sufficient for that, but His miracles were all a preparation for *this,* to show His power and to let His Disciples see He could do all things.

When speaking to the Jews, He said, "This bread which I shall give is My Flesh for the life of the world, for My Flesh is meat indeed and My Blood is drink indeed." He did not say it was a sign of His Body, but His "Flesh indeed." And when the Jews were going from Him, He said: "Doth my words scandalize you? If then you shall see the Son of Man ascend up where He was before," as if He would say, when I do such wonders as these, can anything be impossible to Me? Then turning to His Apostles He said, "Will you also go away?" And Simon Peter answered Him: "Lord, to whom shall we go? Thou hast the words of eternal life." He does not say he understands Him, for the Angels themselves do not comprehend it.

23rd July The test of our love of God is the perfect fulfillment of the law, as measured to us. Hence it becomes obligatory on a Religious not only to observe the commandments, but also the counsels. Christ says, "He that loves Me will keep My words." Each Religious order has attached to it by the direction of God its different duties and rules to be observed, and no matter what great things or great austerities we hear of others practising, 'tis our business to observe and perform exactly the measure of the law as it is given to us by our Rule.

As persons who live in different parts of a kingdom that wish to visit the capital do not follow the same road; being in different places, each will follow the most direct path for him. So it is with the Religious. She is to walk faithfully in the path marked out for her, which is the exact performance of all her duties, attending to time, place, and manner. She should make the love of God the spring of all her duties, and endeavor daily to perfect herself by making frequent acts thereof. She should view Jesus Christ in those she relieves, instructs, converses with, or assists in any way, for He has said, "Amen, I say to you, as long as you did [it] to one of these My least brethern, you did it to Me." In the discharge of her duties, a Religious may often feel a repugnance to do them in the manner pointed out to her; yet if she perseveres, God will reward her an hundred fold, for fidelity is the key to unlock the treasures of Divine love. No occurrence whatever, even the death of relatives, sisters, or anything else, should cause her the least disturbance, or to depart in the least from regular observance.

24th July Jesus Christ in asking His Apostle Peter three times, "Lovest thou Me more than these," wished to impress on our minds the necessity there is, for those who are particularly called to His service, to have this love. If He repeated it but once, we might pass it over too lightly as we are apt to do in many things. The Apostle's being afflicted at His divine Master's question shows us we should even fear that the penetrating eye of God may discover something in even our best actions and dispositions that is not pleasing to Him. It also teaches us that we should diffide in ourselves.

The reason why some derive so little benefit from retreats is they do not continue to put their good resolutions in practice. In vain will they make resolutions and abhor their faults, if they do not apply the remedies, and this is the cause of great disedification. If the retreat should end at night, she ought to say: What resolutions am I to practise tomorrow? What vice am I to endeavor to overcome and virtues to attain? The end we should have in view in making a retreat is to discover what faults we are most subject to or what is the cause of those faults? When we know these, we ought to make strong resolutions to practise the virtues that will enable us to overcome them. All depends on the efforts we make, for although we may have many to correct, yet if we take them singly and apply the proper remedies to each, we shall receive an additional grace for every one we conquer, which in the end will enable us to correct them all.

We must never give up our pursuit of perfection, but labor to arrive at it. St. Paul says, I do not say I am arrived at perfection, but having been called to that state in which I am bound to labor to arrive thereto, I pursue my course daily and force myself to attain to it. This vessel of election does not say he found this practice easy, but he *forced* himself to arrive at it. God who has called us to this state wherein we are bound to aim at perfection, when He sees the efforts we make, will not fail to supply us with grace.

A Religious is bound to contribute as much as possible to the happiness of her community. Circumspection, modesty, and reserve will be remarkable in her who endeavors to do so; equality of manners will be her constant attendants, as much as is in her power and under all circumstances. Circumspection will be so remarkable in her that if anything be said to hurt the feelings of a sister, it can be said she was not the cause of it for she is too circumspect. She will never violate the rule, "Do unto others as you would wish others should do to you."

In saying the Office there may be many words the meaning of which is obscure to us, but we are to discover it is a kind of praise sung by the heavenly citizens, and that they make use of words which we do not understand, and that it is more an act of praise than prayer. Therefore we should unite with them in offering these praises to God, and it would be good at the end of every psalm to say within ourselves, praise be to God!

30th July Be not troubled if anything be said against you, for what is said must be true or false. If true, be not surprised that anyone dare say what you dare do, and endeavor to amend. If false, let it pass. It can do you no harm. You are still the same in God's sight. Bear it patiently; it is better for you than praise.[7]

We should combat vainglory as the greatest obstacle to our salvation. If we are to instruct, visit the sick, or do any other good work, we should offer it to God before we commence, and beg of Him to bestow on us all the graces we stand in need of, for performing it in the manner that will conduce to His greater glory and our eternal salvation. If after this offering, we should feel any secret satisfaction for the good we have done, or in the thanks bestowed on us by those whom we have served, we should not feel the least troubled, but give all the glory to God, and be convinced how necessary this precaution was, as those thoughts truly discover to us our weakness and show to us how much we stand in need of God's grace to preserve us from losing the merit of our actions. Then we might make use of the words Father Avilla [John of Avila] did on a like occasion, "You have come too late; it is already given to God," or with St. Bernard, "I neither began for you, nor will I leave off for you."[8]

There is nothing we require to guard so much against as vainglory. There is not a saint in the calendar but cautions us against it. It is a cunning thief who insinuates itself into our best actions, or like a robber, who meeting a traveller pretends to be going the same way with him, but who on the first opportunity that offers, and when he least expects it, kills him.[9]

Editor's Note

Chapter 3 is dated 1834, has the title "On the same Subject," and contains at least twenty (20) passages that are identical or strongly similar to passages in chapter 2 of the "instructions." Therefore, it is reasonable to assume that the same *archetypes* and *sources* that influenced the content and wording of sections of chapter 2 also influenced the content and wording in the comparable sections in chapter 3. However, chapter 3 (which is shorter than chapter 2) does not contain the passage on "joy and sadness" (at the end of chapter 2), but rather, at its end (July 30), a passage on "vainglory" (not in chapter 2). In this passage, the wording and quotations from St. Gregory (unidentified), St. Bernard, and St. John of Avila are nearly identical to wording in Rodriguez (*Practice,* 1:99, 111), and to wording in Catherine McAuley's handwritten, often paraphrased transcript of parts of this chapter of Rodriguez (her manuscript is numbered CMA/1/5/1 and is preserved in MCA).

CHAPTER 4TH

On the Passion of Jesus Christ

For I have given you an example that as I have done to you, so you do also. —John, ch. 13, v. 15

Behold Jesus Christ washing His disciples' feet. What more humiliating action could He perform? He could descend no lower; His Body is bent to show how our spirit should be bent to everyone, to every humor, and to everything. It was not that we might wash each other's feet that our Saviour did this, but to show us that we are to be humble and condescending to everyone, whether superior, inferior, or equal, and in our own estimation to put ourselves beneath all. "Except you are washed, you shall have no part with Me," as if He would say: "If the instructions I have given you by the instrument I have chosen and in the manner appointed by the Church and approved by Me, do not correct your erroneous worldly notions, change your proud spirit, root up and destroy in your manner, etc., all unbecoming the dignity you aspire to, you shall not be My Spouse. You may go thro' the ceremony of Profession, but I will not acknowledge you; you shall not partake of the happiness promised to the humble, faithful followers of the Lord."[1]

You should therefore, before you go any further, excite lively sentiments of contrition for past transgressions. What means better calculated to effect this than the consideration of the pains and sorrows of Christ?[2] This contrition will produce that hatred of sin that leads to purity of heart and which will attract the eye of God, and will cause Him to unite Himself to you more intimately. He will then manifest Himself so to you, that your heart will be inflamed with love for Him alone; and as resemblance to the beloved object is one of the effects and properties of love, so if you try to resemble Him, it will be a most assured mark whereby you may know if you are among the Spouses of the Lamb. Let your constant study be to form, now more than ever, this resemblance in yourself.

Consider Him in His agony in the garden; reflect what must have been His anguish when it caused blood to flow from the pores in His body; your sins alone were sufficient to make Him suffer this. Endeavor to abhor them now, more than you ever did. Behold Him, shortly after, apprehended and bound to a pillar; to atone for the many irregularities of your tongue and will, He suffered Himself to be thus bound and deprived of liberty. Oh how this should excite you to love Him! Next behold Him struck on the Face; this is considered by the most rational in the world so great an ignominy that they are frequently heard to say, on hearing of some act of violence that at another time would make them shudder, "Oh, they were quite justified in committing it, they could not avoid it, they were provoked to it, they were struck on the face!" Our Saviour endowed His human nature with the most sensitive feelings in order to suffer the more; and therefore, He felt this ignominy in its fullest extent. Conceive, if possible, the enormity of sin which caused the Son of God to submit to this, and resolve every day to become more pleasing to Him, in order that your exertions to destroy, or at least arrest, the progress of this monstrous evil may be more successful.

Behold your Saviour undergoing the cruel scourging, a punishment so degrading that none could be got to inflict it, till they were excited by enlivening their passions and increasing their rage to its utmost height. From this, judge what must be God's rage against sin, when, in order to atone for it, He suffered this punishment to be inflicted on His well-beloved Son. Since one sin alone required this expiation, see how many strokes your sins added to the number.

Consider Him, now carrying His cross to Mt. Calvary with the same meekness and equality of mind that He testified throughout His Passion, and learn to carry the cross you are now going willingly to embrace for love of Him. He makes no exception, no resistance. He is not heard to say, "I am willing to be crucified, but do not place Me between two thieves." Oh No! He utters not a word. Such should be our obedience, and we deprive ourselves of great graces, and the greater part, if not all, the merit of obedience, by making little reserves. We do the thing ordered, but we ask if we may do it in such a place, at such a time, or in such a way. Or we say, "Let me do it entirely! I would rather do it all myself! I do not wish to have an assistant," or "I think such a one would assist me better than the one appointed." We must be most guarded against these or similar exceptions.

Look now to your Redeemer, nailed to the Cross—attached to it so that He could not be separated from it until death released Him. Endeavor to attach yourself to yours in the same way. What is your Cross? When called on to do what is opposed to your judgment, behold your cross! Cling to it, tell your Saviour you will prove to Him your desire to be crucified with Him. When a harsh or unkind expression is used towards you, when an office or employment is given to you for which you feel a repugnance, when you feel disgust or weariness in the performance of daily duties, when, in fine, anything occurs that is painful to your self-love, Oh behold your Cross! Cling to it! See your Redeemer nailed to His; listen to Him telling you that a few years more will put an end to all these troubles and griefs.

Then raise your eyes to the Kingdom He has purchased for you by His Blood. Conceive, if you can, its delights. Look around you; see the beauties of nature, the varieties of plants, flowers, beasts, birds, and fishes. Not a similarity of resemblance exists in any two species. Not two species of birds build their nests in the same way, or support themselves with the same kind of food. Form from this some idea of the power of God, His goodness and love. Reflect that in creating this world He only intended it as a place of pilgrimage, but in Heaven is combined all that His infinite power, goodness, and love could effect to conduce to your happiness. Behold a place and a crown waiting *there* for you. Persevere till the end and *you shall have all.*

From this reflection you cannot hesitate to cry out with your dying and sorrowing Saviour, "Not my will, Heavenly Father, but thine be done!" "Into thy hands I commend my spirit!" From this moment, I give up my conceited judgments, my former spirit, the spirit of esteem, of praise, of impatience, of peevishness, of bitterness, of uncharitableness, of pique, of envy, of jealousy. To Thee, my God, I sacrifice all, and I will adopt in its place the spirit of my Redeemer, particularly His spirit of meekness and humility. I will avoid the least wilful fault, especially against these virtues, for its malice would now be greater and more productive of evil to my soul than it ever was before. In the world it is a common expression, "Do not mind what such a one says, or does; they never think; they never reflect." On the contrary, it is said by them, "I felt very much what such a one said, for he has a reflecting mind. I was surprised a thinking mind would act in such a manner." You see by this that a departure from God's counsels or precepts in a Religious would be far worse than an open violation of God's law in seculars who do not study or think as seriously as they ought on it because they have not received graces or gifts to enable them to do.

Whoever commits a wilful sin renews, as the Apostle tells us, as far as in their power, the sufferings of Jesus Christ. The Religious who would be guilty of a wilful sin or infraction of her Rule, would, it is to be feared, were Jesus Christ to come on earth again, take an active part in putting Him to death. The least deviation from the perfection of your holy state will not fail to give great disedification, and although no remark may escape the lips, yet it will make an impression on the heart and leave in the mind such ideas as, "Oh, after all the meditations and reflections she has made and all the instructions she has received, see how she acts."

On Charity

Fear not, I have redeemed thee, and called thee by name.
Thou art mine. —Isaias 43

1834 The Noviceship is now drawing to a close. We are called on to repose, that is, to lay aside all anxiety, restlessness, straining the mind, servile fear, etc. because God will not bestow the plentitude of His graces where peace and sweetness do not reign in the soul. For peevishness of manner and overanxiety retard the grace of God much more than what might appear greater faults, for this is not walking in the ways of God. When God bestows on us the special grace of vocation to Religious life, He requires of us to form our entire conduct on the example given us by Jesus Christ. This grace of vocation was unmerited on our part. He has left hundreds in the world more deserving, and more likely to correspond with His merciful designs, and, notwithstanding the little efforts as yet made by us to resemble our divine Model, He still continues His graces and is going to crown all by making us the Spouses of His Son.

Let us then give Him our hearts with all their affections, and commence in earnest to form yourselves according to the image of our Divine Model. Behold Him stripped of His garments and clothed with others to make Him an object of derision to the spectators. He is struck on one cheek, and He presents the other. His cherished Apostles, whom He had fostered with so much care and to whom He had given such frequent instructions, all forsook and abandoned Him. Yet not an impatient word, not a heartbroken expression such as "Oh, this is too bad, how can I bear this?" escapes Him. Not a sigh is heard, not even an annoyed or perplexed look can be perceived.

When an affair in which we are engaged fails, when in the discharge of duties we meet with what may be considered perplexing difficulties, and after using our best efforts we cannot effect what we wish; when after laboring to correct in others what is remiss or disorderly, our efforts appear fruitless, our labors lost, and our instructions thrown away, what care should we take not to let even a disturbed motion arise, nor even a look of suppressed annoyance appear. All should be as calm, as undisturbed, as if everything had gone on to our wishes. Better, a thousand times better, would it be to suffer losses, even to feel want, than to let one overanxious, perplexed feeling be observed. This would be showing more of a worldly spirit than if we were to go out to a tea party.

We are selected to promote the glory of God, and every movement in us should tend to this noble end. For this purpose we must withdraw our hearts and minds from all created objects. By this we are to understand not only visible and created objects, but also the creations of our imaginations, such as groundless fear and anxieties, scruples, etc. To embrace Religious life is sovereign perfection, superior to and above everything human, but to live in Religion without supporting the dignity of the state is deplorable misfortune, and leads to ultimate ruin. To support this dignity of our state we should everyday of our life, though this were a space of a hundred years, labor so to advance in perfection as to be able to say each night, "Well, I hope I am now more deserving of God's love than I ever was before."

Religion is a state admitting of no variety, but presents a sickening sameness if not animated and enlivened by fervor. Let us now recall our first fervor, and not be discouraged by the sight of passions we have still to subdue. God who has called us to our holy state will give us His supporting and enlivening grace to persevere in it, if we labor to subdue passion and self will. By the word "passion" here we are not to understand it as it is generally applied in the world. Passion, for instance, in a Religious is fondness for our own opinion, an uneasiness when it is not adopted, and so of other things. We must so detach ourselves from ourselves and from everything else that is not God, as to be able to view such things and practices as are approved of in the Convent, yet quite opposed to our own ideas and opinions, without one disturbed motion arising or costing us one perplexing thought.

Then it is, God will form a close union with us, and bestow

on us new and supporting grace which will preserve in us *that* fervor which renders religion a paradise, the delights of which are unknown to the tepid soul. This labor is to be calm and undisturbed, the fruit of serious application, not a wearisome toil. We must, at this time, regulate every affection, rooting out what is inordinate, loving only for and in God. And even these affections that are properly regulated must be, for the present, suspended, and not a moment given to them. All must be for God and whatever is connected with the alliance He is going to form with us. Fervor may be maintained by frequent acts of the love of God made with a sincere heart, though without sensible devotion, which will enable us to remain calm and undisturbed in the most distressing calamities.

Section 1: Poverty

The Vow of Poverty is considered by Divines a second baptism, purifying the person who makes it from all sin. What makes this Vow so meritorious before God is that by it we renounced not only that which we actually possessed but all that we might hereafter possess. By it we deprive ourselves of the possibility of possessing anything during life. It is not so much what we renounce as the act of renunciation that makes it meritorious, so that a person possessing little or no property merits as much as another having great riches, because she renounces the power of possessing, the power of having authority and of being her own mistress, which are so strongly rooted in the heart that persons in the lowest stations of life would not yield them up for anything that could be offered them.

A Religious who has the true spirit of poverty will be indifferent as to what she eats, drinks, or wears, desiring nothing but what is set before her, equally happy when the poorest fare is given her as if it were the greatest luxury. If these feelings actuate her, she need not fear infringing on her Vow of Poverty by wearing what is costly, or eating what is dainty, when presented to her. The person called a labourer, a poor man in the world, may very often be in comfortable circumstances, a stranger to what want is. Still he is not his own master; he must attend the bell when it calls him to labour. He cannot say, "I'll go when I am more disposed, when I rest a little longer." Oh no, this liberty of acting according to his own will he is deprived of, by his condition. So it is with the Religious. By making a Vow of Poverty, she deprived herself of the liberty of free will. She must rise when called; if not, she deprives herself of graces. If she makes a reserve in her renunciation, she cannot be said to be perfectly poor. See the extent, the value of this Vow. See what makes it so acceptable to God. In making the Vow of Poverty, you do not know what misery, what want, you may hereafter be exposed to. Perhaps the house you live in may be burned, or plundered by robbers, or destroyed by the enemies of our Faith, and you, with the rest of the Community, thrown on the world to beg your subsistence.

It is right and approved of by all, that we understand the value of the offering we are going to make to God by the Vow of Poverty, and although we must feel [that] it falls infinitely short of what we receive in return, still when we give all we have, all that nature holds dearest, with a generous heart, it will be before God as if it were equivalent to what He will bestow on us. This offering should be renewed frequently, especially when we feel any desire or wish for these little gratifications which nature craves, and which in themselves are quite harmless and may be lawfully indulged in by good people in the world. Oh! let us not, on those occasions, forget to remind God, as it were, that for love of

Him we have deprived ourselves of them. This manner of acting is considered by spiritual wits more pleasing to God than if we were to say, "I never cared for such or such things! I never enjoyed them. I do not feel any loss for them!" "I have purified you," says Jesus Christ, "in the furnace of poverty, that is, by depriving you of all temporal goods, which are the sources of all sin, I have withdrawn you from its snares." When we consider the evils entailed by sin, how grateful should we feel for being withdrawn from its greatest incentive!

Poverty also enables us to acquire all virtues. It illuminates the mind and draws us nearer to that cherished virtue of our dear Redeemer, *humility*. By embracing Poverty we practise the four cardinal virtues in so eminent a degree that we need not fear anymore to transgress them. It also leads to union with God. The more the heart is withdrawn from earthly things, the easier it finds access to God. But let us understand well what true poverty is. To be poor in spirit does not consist in wearing poor clothes, and yet at the same time be covetous—covetous of praise, of preferment, of distinction. To be poor in spirit we must be dead to those things.

We must be what the world terms mean-spirited. If an unkind or mortifying word is said of, or anything done to us, that in the world would be considered an affront and to resent it deemed quite justifiable, we must be as a dead body that remains unmoved and insensible under the most cruel treatment, and act as if we had no feeling so that the most discerning could see by our countenance that no anxiety or uneasiness was felt, except for the person so acting, fearing they had displeased God. If we would be poor, according to Jesus Christ, it is thus we must act so as to be able to say, "My heart and my body hath failed me. Thou, Oh Lord, art my power and my glory." It will not be difficult to bring ourselves to these feelings if we reflect how we really are before God, our total dependence on Him, our offenses against Him continually calling out for justice, our abuse of graces received, and the many more of which we have been deprived in consequence of such abuses, etc.

Poverty also withdraws us from the many evils attendant on riches, [such] as solicitudes, pains, anxieties, etc. When the heart is suffered to become attached to those, it is incredible with what force it clings to them, so much so that the loss of them sometimes costs life. This love of riches is ingrafted in our nature, nor is it the greatness of the loss or the want occasioned thereby that causes disquiet, but the attachment of the heart. For the poor person will bemoan his few pounds saved, though in no want of them, and the rich man, though abounding in wealth, will lose his peace of mind when [he] fails in any project likely to add to his superabundance. Thus it is not riches, but the attachment to them that is injurious. Now to possess them without being attached to them is extremely difficult, and here we see what we owe to God for having withdrawn us from the evil and danger of riches, and given us grace to embrace a state where no impediment obstructs our hearts from attaching themselves to God alone, no solicitude exists except for God and His glory, and these are ever accompanied with peace, happiness, and joy.

"Seek first the kingdom of God and His justice"—this is our motto. If we are told of the illness of our dearest friends, we enquire with earnestness if all spiritual aid is afforded them, or could we in any way contribute to it? This done, we have no further solicitude, no concern but for what regards God. If we do not seek humiliations and mortifications, at least when they come we should receive them with joy and gratitude because we seek but the kingdom of God, and we know these are so many helps to attain it. In a word, we are lord and master over riches, as St. John Climacus observes, "Having nothing, yet possessing all things."[3]

A Religious who has divested herself of every attachment but God, that feels no solicitude but for what concerns His glory, will contribute more to His honor and the interests of Religion in her intercourse with seculars, than by all the good works she could perform during her life. The feeling that influences her will be visible in her demeanour. If anything is mentioned that tends not to God or His glory, she will listen to it with indifferent attention, but let the subject regard God, she immediately becomes animated and interested, and the most irreligious secular will go away from her edified, and say, "This Religious has truly given up the world."

Let us now see the rewards promised to poverty. We should always remember that poverty principally consists in total renunciation and detachment from everything but God, and that there would be more danger of sinning against this Vow by refusing to partake of the greatest luxury when set before us, than by partaking of it, for a beggar will not refuse a nice or dainty thing when given, but receives it thankfully, and with gratitude will receive a cold potato. We should act after the same manner.

"Amen, I say to you, you who have left father or mother, or house or land, for My Name's sake, shall receive a hundred fold in this life, and in the world to come life everlasting." Here is a solemn promise from the mouth of Truth Itself; He has made the contract; if we fulfill our part, He will consider Himself our debtor. Again He says, "Amen, I say to you, that you who have left all to follow Me, shall sit [on] thrones judging the twelve tribes of Israel." Oh, what honor, what power, but this exaltation will not affect us as earthly distinctions would; we will not glory that we are above others, but that we are near to God and that He is pleased with us. And as persons placed in the rank of judging on earth generally possess great influence in the state, so we also may hope to have influence with God.

How this consideration should incite us to give up every attachment for the dearest and most beloved friends that we then may make interest for them. Even here, the more pleasing we are to God, the more favorably will He hear our prayers, and bestow on those for whom we petition more graces and blessings, so that we can do more for them in a short time than we would be able to do during our lives if not detached and holy. We would be very miserable indeed if such favors did not excite us to cry out: "What shall I render to the Lord for all the good things He hath given me?"

Let us offer a heart overflowing with gratitude and love, full of vigour to do anything and everything His will manifests. Let this feeling be visible in our demeanour at all times, and thus speak more than words could express. Let us forever banish from us that cold, calculated, and measured piety which is unworthy a grateful heart truly sensible of the signal favors bestowed on it. Let us make the world sensible of these favors, and make Religion appear what it really is, sweet, amiable, and attractive.

By vowing to observe poverty we enhance its merit before God, far beyond the most rigid poverty practised in the world, because we deprive ourselves of the power and liberty of changing from this state during our lives without incurring the guilt of mortal sin. We oblige ourselves to possess nothing, to receive nothing, to dispose of nothing, without permission. This is in this sense that we are to become little children. The will, judgment, and faculties of mind and body are here sacrificed. This Vow is considered the basis and foundation of religious life, for if perfectly practised, it will root up every vice and imperfection. Before making it, we call on God and His Servants in Heaven and on earth to witness it, and afterwards we say aloud: "I have chosen to be an abject in the house of my God." Oh, how inconsistent, how irreconcilable, to hear the same Religious say after, "I cannot bear this, I did not think a Sister or Mother would act in such a manner, I was greatly hurt, my feelings were greatly wounded," etc.

You have chosen to be an abject, a poor mean creature, a nothing, that considers everyone above her, who blushes if brought into notice, and stares in amazement if her opinion is asked. Such are at least the effects that poverty produces. The spirit is subdued, we become insensible to affronts, and consider ourselves happy in any miserable corner, unknown and unnoticed. See what you have chosen in the house of God, your portion. How are you to know the sincerity of your heart if you are never put to the test? Your world is the house you live in, where God will always permit you to be exercised, and until you find in yourself a perfect image of this description of an abject Religious, you cannot suppose you have attained the perfection of poverty.

The 1st virtue inseparable from poverty is humility. This will produce a meek, gentle, unassuming demeanor. No authoritative, arrogant, mistress-like expression should be heard from a Religious who makes a Vow of Poverty. If obliged to exercise authority, which is sometimes indispensable, it should be in such a manner as to convince the person over whom it is exercised that it is painful. If we have to refuse a demand, it is to be done decidedly, but mildly, showing the impossibility of according it, or that it would not be advantageous, and let it always be seen that we would feel much happier if we could yield to the request.

Patience is the 2nd virtue we must acquire to become truly

poor. We know not to what extremities we may hereafter be reduced. We may not be able to enjoy the comforts we now have; we may not even have what is necessary to support nature. We should therefore prepare our minds for this (for it may happen), and be willing to meet every privation not only with patience, but provided the poor did not suffer, nor God's glory be less promoted, with joy and delight.

The 3rd virtue attendant on poverty is labor, which principally consists in the performance of mean and servile offices. We should let no day pass without doing something of this kind, and although they may not be more than we would have done in the world, their merit before God is widely different. In the world we would have worked so from whim, choice, or inclination, not with an intention of always continuing to do so, but in Religion we bind ourselves to this labor; we embrace it for the love of God, and that we may more closely resemble Jesus Christ. We try to imitate Him in discharging it, doing as we would have done it had He in person overlooked it.

Let us now consider the poverty Jesus Christ manifests in the Blessed Sacrament, that we may thereby be drawn to the practice of it for the love of Him, remembering that we are placed in a place of pasture, so the fruit we draw from our Communions should be much greater than that of those placed in the world. No act of our Saviour's more clearly shows what He was, nor what He wished us to be, than the institution of the Blessed Eucharist. He conceals Himself under the plainest and simplest materials, which He knew could always be had without difficulty or expense. He submits Himself to be lodged in the poorest cabin as easily as in a tabernacle of gold. The simple words of consecration effect the change! No pomp, no grandeur, no ornament, no science is here displayed. All the exterior grandeur and ceremonies that now accompany the Holy Sacrifice have been introduced by the Church, in reverence to Him and to prevent the possibility of our doubting the Mystery because of the simplicity of the style.

We cannot love this Divine Saviour without loving poverty, His dear and cherished virtue. By this Vow we are called upon, not only to renounce the possession, but even the shadow of propriety of any earthly goods; that is, we ought in our intercourse with the sisters avoid any expression such as, "I'll get it for you, I'll ask it for you," because this appears as if you supposed you had more in your power and influence to obtain them than they had. It is much safer and much more like a poor Religious to say, "Ah! cannot you ask yourself; you will obtain it as soon as I would." Though we should, at all times, be in a disposition to oblige everyone, we never should make ourselves remarkable for doing so. What is most recommended is to be noticed only for *not being noticeable.*

The Vow of Poverty does not oblige us to be indifferent to what we eat. We can observe it in its perfection and even relish and like what is set before us, but we should not wish for anything else, nor to have it at any other time, nor served in any other manner, and we should have our minds disposed to feel the want of necessary subsistence, if it please God to reduce us to such extremities. But poverty also obliges us to renounce every title to honors, pleasures and conveniences, spending our time as industriously as if we were obliged to earn our subsistence, uniting ourselves familiarly to contempt and indigence, not feeling the least surprised or hurt at any slight put on us. For some persons in the world look upon us as poor wretches and consider the act of retiring from the world as the effects of a low, mean spirit, and even degenerating from what God intended us to be. We should, therefore, glory in being regarded in this light.

We have also sworn by the Vow of Poverty to renounce pride, that is, a desire or wish to be considered something more than the rest of the Sisters, as to possess more influence, more knowledge, more talent, more piety, more, in fine, of anything than another Sister. If this feeling of self-sufficiency or pride reigns in us, it will manifest itself in our conduct and manners, and be productive of incalculable evil, which is the strongest proof that it is opposed to and entirely inconsistent with evangelical poverty.

We have also sworn to renounce interior presumption, that is, a consciousness that we could undertake to do things that another sister would have no business to attempt; that we could do such or such a thing much better than it is done by others; that we could [fill] such an office with the greatest ease, and cannot see why others find such difficulty in it. Oh! may God preserve us from this pernicious evil. We should always be firmly persuaded that everything is done much better than we could perform it, and then the necessary aid, for accomplishing whatever is allotted us, will not be withdrawn by God, who resists the proud and gives His grace to the humble.

Section 2: Chastity

The surest means to preserve the Vow of Chastity is disengagement from creatures and mortification of the senses; without this, it is difficult to preserve it as a Religious should. We must banish from our minds all anxiety to know what has become of such or such a one, how they are going on, where they are, etc. Now at first, it will appear that such enquiries will not endanger purity of heart, but they do. They are very often the cause of our hearing things that will be dangerous for us, and which we should be strangers to. We must restrain the eyes, the ears, the tongue, the palate. All must be continually mortified to preserve the mind and heart pure. Attachment to the pleasures of sense and irregular passions are as a thick cloud which conceal[s] the Sun of Justice from the soul. Any deviation from the perfection of our state is called an irregular passion; for example, if we read a letter and then read it a second time to indulge a selfish feeling, this is an irregular passion. If we see such a thing, or such a one, we seek by every means to know their business, and what the thing is for, this is also an irregular passion and something like curiosity.

Our lives must resemble Angels in conversation, in dwelling, and in purity. Our soul is as a mirror, susceptible of the slightest stain. It is incredible what a trifling thing in the look, manner, words, or even gait of a Religious will scandalize a secular. An incautious word, an anxious look, or enquiry about anything worldly, a light gaiety of manner, would make them say, "Oh, dear me, I did not think a Nun would say that, I did not think she cared for such things. She is not at all what I supposed a Religious ought to be," etc. Thus she makes an impression prejudicial to the glory of God, that may never be effaced. To avoid this evil we must labor continually. It will not do to say, "I will act in such a manner." Oh no! we must struggle to make ourselves act in the manner we know we ought. The Sisters who say they will do what they will not struggle to make themselves do will never do what they ought. Neither must we be satisfied after having once, or twice, or even a hundred times, acted right. We should not say, "Oh, now, surely I need not be so much on my guard. I am an adept, now I do not require to be watching every word, every movement, every gesture lest I should disedify seculars." Never to our last breath can we speak thus, for after our best efforts we will find something to restrain or correct.

It would be a most dangerous error for a Religious to suppose she observed her Vow of Chastity by merely avoiding every sin against purity. She would be very ignorant indeed of her obligations, if she thought that was all that was required of her. To observe it faithfully, she must be a chaste resemblance of her Divine Spouse, that is, a perfect likeness of Him, so that all who converse or associate with her may find in her what they would have seen in Jesus Christ when on earth. Patient, forbearing, charitable, as He was, no volatile manners, no flow of words, no useless expressions, nothing unbecoming, nothing trifling, no hurried step, no hasty expression, always meek under every circumstance, even the most painful and undeserved, her countenance always pleasing to behold, her temper ever the same, ever amiable, ever sweet, a constant equality ever reigning in her mind so that no accident could disturb it. Behold the portrait you are to resemble that you may be considered truly chaste by your all-wise and all seeing Judge.

By the Vow of Chastity we are closely united to the Incarnate Word; our actions and words should therefore proclaim this high dignity. It would, therefore, be very unbecoming in a Religious to extol the state of Matrimony. It is a holy state, no doubt, but the Religious is incomparably more perfect. Jesus Christ has given *it* the most decided preference. Let us therefore leave it to the pastors of the Church to extol the one, but it is for us to proclaim the sanctity of the other, and never to seem unmindful or ungrateful for the high favor done us of being called to it.

We cannot better describe the spiritual union you are going to contract with Jesus Christ, than by representing it under the form of union contracted by matrimony. In order to be happy, there must be a communication of goods; no separate interests, views, or profits can exist. Of two they become but one—one heart, one sentiment seem to animate both. What one thinks, both think. What one wishes, the other desires. Hence it is always observed that when any property is settled on one over which the other has no control, this happiness never exists between them. There is an entire surrender of the will and affections, so that both parties united are at all times ready to be separated from the whole world rather than from each other. Nor is this at all considered unnatural. The fondest and most attached parents are heard to say, "Ah, she will not fret at leaving us when she is not separated from him." We cannot wonder at this, so strong, so indissoluble is the attachment that is formed by the bond of matrimony.

The union you are going to contract should be much stronger, for grace is far above nature. The one is a natural union, but yours is supernatural. Your heart should be at all times so disposed as to be willing to be separated from everyone and from everything so as to do the will of your Spouse. And where you feel a repugnance in yourself to do this, you may be assured you have an irregular affection for the person or thing that causes this sensation, which is quite opposed to your holy state, and until this is rooted out of your heart you will never enjoy the plentitude of graces bestowed on those who empty their hearts of everything that Jesus Christ alone may fill them. It is not wrong to have an affection for our friends, but the love of God should be paramount in us. Then it is that attached to nothing but Him, we will meet with courage every difficulty, and as where there is love, there is no labor, so those things that are in themselves mortifying, painful, and irksome will be to us not only tolerable but even sweet and pleasant.

Section 3: Obedience

The third means by which we are to form this union with God is the Vow of Obedience, which chiefly constitutes the Religious Life. The other Vows may [be], and often are, practised by persons in the world, but this Vow never can. By the other two, we offer what appertains to the body, but by this we sacrifice the will and understanding, the noblest faculties of the soul, which consequently render this Vow more agreeable and meritorious before God. To attain its perfection we ought, when occasion offers, yield our will and judgment to those of our equals, in order that we may acquire the same perfect submission to our Superiors. There is no sacrifice more painful to nature than this, for the love of one's own will, opinion, or judgment is so deeply engrafted in the heart that we see children, pure and innocent, quarrel and dispute to maintain them. Our Saviour, knowing that all evil takes its rise from the inequality of the will and judgment, says, "He that will be My disciple, let him deny himself, take up his cross and follow Me," as if He would say, "Here is the Model I give you, for your imitation. You must be obedient as I was, even to death, but remember, in order to do so, you must take up your cross. You will always feel its weight, but I will always support you under it."

The 1st prerogative of obedience is that by it we substitute the Will of God for the will of man. By it we know what God would have us do, more certainly than if an angel descended from heaven to announce it to us. In having no will but the Will of God manifested to us by our Superiors, we become closely united to Him. He says Himself that He prefers it to holocausts and sacrifices. We should take care to perform our acts of obedience for the love of God. Obedience gives great glory to God, for by it the noblest part of the noblest work of creation is consecrated to Him. If we are influenced in our Obedience by affection for the person who commands, or because she has an affection for us, because we consider her judgment superior to us, because we know she has more talent, experience, etc., then we have no merit for our obedience before God.

In order that our obedience be perfectly pleasing to Him, we must obey against our reason. As a signal mark that God expects this from those whom He calls to live under obedience, it invariably happens that an ill-judged thing performed through obedience and against the reason of the person who performs it, turns out better and is more productive of good than the wisest and most prudent undertaking when contrary to obedience. A kind of miracle is thus worked, to prove the excellence of obedience. It is by the constant practice of it that we will enjoy its delights, and experience the truth of these words: "My yoke is sweet and My burden light." Oh glorious advantage of obedience, which elevates the meanest action to a high degree of glory, and gives in every doubt and difficulty immediate and free access to God. For on consulting our Superiors, we may feel as happy and as convinced that what they say or think is what God would say or think if it were possible we could see Him and hear Him speak to us, for the words "He that hears you hears Me" are addressed to all Religious Superiors. And as by faith you feel assured that when the priest pronounces over you the words of absolution the guilt of sin is remitted, if you have brought to the sacred tribunal the necessary dispositions, so should you, with the same lively faith, hear and abide by the decisions of every Religious Superior appointed by the Church for your government.

Section 4: Charity

The effect Meditation should produce in you is to render you as a lamp consumed with the fire of divine love, shining and giving light to all. If the love of God really reigns in your heart, it will quickly show itself in the exterior. You will become sweet and attractive in your manner. You will have a tender esteem for your Sisters and for everyone, beholding in them the image of God. This will prevent every harsh, cold or bitter expression. If you have to correct, it will be visible that it is painful for you to do so; if an untoward circumstance happens, you will bear it with a happy patience, so that those looking on will see something in you that is not to be met with in the world. You have zeal for God's glory, but it will be a cheerful, animating zeal, not sullen or gloomy. We may hold it for certain that meekness and gentleness on all occasions, with all persons and under every circumstance, will be more productive of good than any other method we could possibly adopt.

This universal mildness belongs peculiarly to the religious state, and, as it were, to prove this, where it is not exercised Almighty God withholds His blessing; consequently no good can be expected. You desire to promote the glory of God and your neighbour's salvation. Reflect then, how contrary to this it would be to hear you say, "I told you not to do that. I knew you would do it wrong," or "I told her twenty times to do it in such a manner, and she will not." Oh, it is most grievous to hear a Religious make use of this sharp, bitter, worldly language. The persons to whom you thus express yourself will lose their esteem for you, and consequently you cannot promote their spiritual good. On the contrary, if you thus express yourself, "I am sure you forgot, or you would not have done so." "Oh, now won't you in future do so and so," such kind expressions, united to the circumstances of being ever ready to excuse them, will draw their esteem and respect. They will do anything for you, and whatever you say to them for their spiritual good will sink deep into their hearts, and perhaps when you are in your grave will produce abundant fruit. They will, in fine, give praise to God and be ever ready to defend the cause of Religious, saying, "They never found in the world such persons as they met with in the Convent."

If you really love God, you will thus prove it, for the proof of love is deeds.[4] You have disengaged yourself from worldly goods. How absurd would it be to hear you say, "I brought such and such to this house. My friends and connections are valuable to the Institute." If you have not brought virtue with you, or at least, if you are not endeavoring to acquire it, you have brought nothing. Though you had thousands, what is it? Vanity and smoke! The sister who is virtuous, mild, sweet, and unassuming, though she possess not a penny, is truly valuable. The sister destitute of these qualities, though she possessed millions, is quite valueless, and better a thousand times would it be for the Institute that she had never entered it. The sister who discharges the most arduous offices in the Convent, but in a worldly, hurried, important manner, is an injury to the Convent, while one who is not capable of fulfilling any office, but by her sweetness and amiability gives general edification is a treasure.

If we saw any creature raised to high dignity, wealth, power, etc., we would consider it an honor to be noticed by him, and think it presumptuous to say we loved him. Oh how infinitely honored are we then in being permitted to love the King of kings. Could anyone be so insensible, so infatuated, as not to avail themselves of such an honor? If we love God, we will undoubtedly love our neighbour also; they are as cause and effect.

Jesus Christ counsels us to love our neighbour as ourselves. Now nothing is more certain than that we desire for every spiritual advantage, and we love everything that contributes to it. Then to fulfil this command, we should, with equal ardour, desire the same for our neighbour. In vain do we say we love our sisters if we do not show by our acts we truly love them. As it is impossible to love God without manifesting a love for our neighbour, so it is equally impossible to love our neighbour without manifesting it in our conduct. For as long as we are in these miserable bodies we must show by acts our feelings. How often are persons heard to say, "I do not think such a person likes me." On being answered, they do, they reply, "I would never suppose so from her manner." To see this more closely, we have only to observe every writing or instruction given by spiritual fathers, which often costs them labor and tears, that whenever they speak of union and charity, they do so decidedly, and in such words as these—banish from your heart all coldness, aversion, and reserve—hereby showing that it is not sufficient not to dislike our sisters in our hearts, but that we must have a warm, cordial affection for all, and manifest it by words, actions and manners. In fine, our charity must be in our hearts, and from our hearts, and a charity such as Jesus Christ practised whilst on earth, who to let us see how much He desired to establish this charity amongst His chosen ones, reserved it for His last discourse, and, as it were, dying injunction, "Love one another as I have loved you."

The words of a parent or friend, when about to leave us, never fail to make a lasting impression, and have been known to effect the greatest conversions and changes. How often may we hear it said, "Oh it was their dying request. I must fulfil it." Is it then to the dying request of a God Man that we will only be insensible? Let us now resolve to comply with this, in its fullest extent. Ah, never let such expressions as these be heard amongst us: "Do as you like, it is nothing to me! Let such a sister do it, she will do it better than I!" Oh how far removed from true charity are these words and ideas! If we indulge in them, we may expect that Jesus Christ will feel towards us as an affectionate, fond mother would feel towards a person who would say, "I love you very much, but I dislike your child." Doubtless this mother would despise such love, and would not entertain one spark of affection for it.

True charity is invincible to coldness or ingratitude. Although some sisters may not have those qualities that attract esteem and love, though they may even be cold and reserved, yet this will not exempt us from exercising kind and cordial charity towards them. We cannot say, "I will be stiff towards such a sister because she is stiff to me." Oh no! On the contrary, we should, as it were, force this sister to become amiable by the sweet attractiveness of our manners. Acting otherwise, we will not be imitating the charity of Jesus Christ. He does not say, "I must withhold my graces from you. I cannot admit you to My sacraments, you are so unfaithful to them." Oh no! His greatest care is to make the soul return to Him. Even our greatest ingratitude does not cool His love for us. It may be difficult for us to act thus at times, but the example of Jesus Christ will render it pleasing and delightful. All spiritual writers agree that this well ordered charity begins at home. Hence, if we indulge any coldness or pique towards our sisters, though we were to perform the most heroic deeds of charity towards our neighbour, though the city were in admiration of our works, our charity will be imperfect, wanting what is essential to render our works pleasing to God, that is, charity of the mind and heart. Without this our labors will be as froth before God, void of all merit.

Our Saviour Who, as it were, formed the first Religious Community that existed on earth, knowing the impossibility of its continuance without unanimity and cordial charity, constantly inculcated it. He says, "This is My commandment, that you love one another as I have loved you." This charity is the Queen of virtues. Where it reigns, every virtue flourishes; it banishes detraction, murmurings, suspicions, and rash judgments. Where it dwells, God also dwells; where *it does not exist, God cannot be.* The sister who does not practise this charity undermines as far as in her power our Institute, whilst the sweet, meek, charitable sister attracts the eye of God, and draws His blessings on the Convent in which she dwells. Thanks then to God, everyone has it in her power to increase religion.

Our charity to be perfect should be well ordered, that is, it should be a respectful charity shown to all, especially to those who hold the principal offices in the house. This is necessary for the preservation of order, and should it happen that a junior sister, inferior to you in talent, judgment, or experience, be raised to office while you are unnoticed, if you possess true charity you will delight in exercising towards this sister the respect due to her on account of her office, and which is indispensable for the preservation of well ordered charity. If she were superior to you in every way, you would no doubt respect her from a sense of her superiority. This you would do were you in the world, but the love of God being the spring that should actuate you in religion, you should feel more happy in proving your love by respecting for His Sake the person on whom you might look with contempt in the world. Besides, your example will powerfully influence younger sisters. Thus you will be instrumental in preserving that order which constitutes the beauty of religion, and which attracts the eye of the God of order and regularity.

If you would be perfectly charitable, remove every obstacle

to becoming so. If a suspicion, an unkind thought, a coldness towards any sister, enter your mind, banish it instantly; fly from it as you would from poison. Act thus and you will remove the greatest impediments to perfect charity. Seek no distinctions or singularities. Do not suppose that because you are professed, that to keep up your dignity, it is necessary to show disapprobation of everything in the conduct and manners of young sisters that appears to you derogatory to the Religious state. This idea would be very erroneous and quite opposed to your duty. You will support your dignity of professed sister much better by observing towards younger sisters a sweet, kind demeanor, which will attract, and make them long for the moment they are to pronounce their vows, that *they* may *then* become the amiable sister you appear to them to be.

Members of the same body, we should all partake of the griefs and joys of each other; if good is effected by one, the others should rejoice, as if it were themselves did it, for "Charity envieth not." When tempted to be cold or stiff with a sister, we should ask ourselves this question: If the others treated her as I do, could it be possible she or anyone else would persevere in religion? No, it would be so afflicting that human nature could not endure it. Zeal for the salvation of souls should be an effect of this charity, and how could you better exercise it than in attracting souls to form that union with God that the Religious Profession presupposes? Therefore remember, well-ordered charity begins at home. It is the most divine of all divine things, to labor for the salvation of souls; it is, as it were, gathering the scattered drops of Blood that were shed on Calvary; it is adding brilliant jewels to the Crown of our Saviour, for to save souls is His joy and His crown. He tells us that it was the zeal that consumed Him, that rendered Him so pleasing to His Eternal Father.

Your zeal to be efficacious should be tender, charitable, and prudent, that is, you must have energy, but it should be tempered by sweetness. It is not true zeal to satisfy yourself with saying, "I did my duty. I read for them." Oh no! There must be an earnest solicitude felt, and shown, for those under your care. You must pray, entreat, beseech, and not cease while a breath of life remains, until you have the Infinite merits of Christ applied to the soul of the sinner by means of the Sacraments; in fine, you must on this occasion act in the same manner as you would towards your dearest friends for whose eternal welfare you would willingly sacrifice your life. But sweetness and tenderness should also accompany this earnestness.

Zeal is also to be humble, feeling yourself unworthy so noble an employment as that of laboring for their salvation, and to be convinced that all your efforts, without the grace of God, will be unavailing. If you are humble, you will not feel disturbed when your efforts are unsuccessful. Intimate union with God is essential, that your zeal may be fruitful. First, for we have pledged ourselves solemnly to attain sanctity, which presupposes this union. Secondly, how can we infuse into others what we ourselves do not possess? How can we teach the love of God when our own hearts are cold? And thirdly, prayer and recollection, which will not be found where this union does not exist. These are more powerful means to attain the good we labor for than the most eloquent, lengthened, and persuasive discourses. If then we thirst for the salvation of souls, let us labor for our own sanctification, and remember, as it is a labor, it is not to be acquired without struggles and vigorous efforts.

Prayer, retirement, and recollection are not sufficient for those who are called upon to labor for the salvation of souls. They should be like the angels who, while fulfilling the office of guardians, lose not for a moment the presence of God, or as the compass which goes round its circle without stirring from its centre. Now our centre is God, from Whom all our actions should spring as from their source, and no exterior action ought to separate us from Him.[5]

The functions of Martha should be for Him as well as the Choir duties. It is want of attention to this important point that causes these duties to be distracting to us, and when engaged in them, we require to watch ourselves more than when praying, for in this we are calm and collected, both of which lead to God, while the former are calculated to withdraw us from Him, for Whom all things should be done. He requires that we should be shining lamps, giving light to all around us, and how are we to do this if not by the manner in which we discharge the duties of Martha?[6]

Editor's Note

The main *archetype* underlying most of chapter 4 is the Naas manuscript titled "Instructions before Profession," numbered C9/4/5, and preserved in Naas Box C9 at MCA. This manuscript often has nearly identical wording to parts of chapter 4, especially in the sections devoted to poverty, chastity, and charity, sections which are also, in many instances, similar to corresponding sections of chapter 1. Both chapter 1 and chapter 4 are apparently addressed to novices preparing for their profession of religious vows. At the beginning of the first long section "On Charity" in chapter 4 the year "1834" is given. While no year is given for that section in chapter 1, those instructions could not have occurred before late 1832 or early 1833 (when the first Baggot Street profession ceremony occurred). See Editor's Note to chapter 2 for a discussion of the probable origin of the Naas manuscripts.

Part 2: Instructions

The primary *source* for the general content of chapter 4 is apparently Rodriguez, *Practice,* especially vols. 2 and 3. Sometimes the language in chapter 4 is identical to Rodriguez's; more often it is a paraphrase of his thought. Where the correspondences seem particularly striking, abbreviated quotations of Rodriguez's text are given in the notes. One might also wish to consult the notes to chapter 1, since some passages in that chapter are similar in content or wording to passages in chapter 4. Elsewhere in this chapter, references to Bourdaloue, *Spiritual Retreat for Religious Persons;* Marin, *Perfect Religious;* and Luis de Granada, *Sinner's Guide,* are cited as possible sources for specific images or content.

CHAPTER [5TH]

Remarks on some Chapters of our Holy Rule

Hear, O Israel! and observe the precepts which the Lord your God commanded that I should teach you. . . . Lay up these my words in your hearts and minds, and hang them for a sign on your hands, and place them between your eyes. —[Deut. 6:1, 6, 8]

The Rule is what contains the law;[1] the Constitutions are the regulations made by the constituted authorities for fulfilling the Law into force, in the manner which seems best to them, and which is in their power to change or dispense with, according to circumstances. For example, the Rule ordains the observance of silence; the Constitutions point out the time and manner in which it is to be observed.

A Sister in making her Vows does not vow to perform any particular duty, but she binds herself to the Institute in which she knows these duties are performed, yet not to any one in particular. A sister no more forfeits her claim of fidelity to her sacred engagements than a mother would who felt a great dislike to teaching her children their lessons, yet saw [that] they were perfectly taught them by others. In the same way, every sister should desire and have in view the well performance of the various duties of the Institute, but it does not follow that each one is to perform them all. It is not necessary that all the Sisters should have the same employments, or like them.

The words of our Holy Rule, Chapter 1st, Sec. 1st are "should also have in view what is peculiarly characteristic of this Congregation, that is, the most assiduous application to the Instruction of poor girls, the Visitation of the sick, and the protection of distressed women of good character."[2] That is, that all these duties are to be discharged by the Sisters appointed to each one, for occupations are given by Superiors according to each one's talents and capabilities. Our Saviour would not be displeased if He were on earth, and if we said to Him, "I would prefer being employed in this duty rather than in another," but to act on this feeling would incur His displeasure.

Although in the approbation it says that the "Rules shall not oblige under pain of sin, mortal or venial, except where the transgression of any article is a violation of the Vows, or is in itself a sin independently of the Rule,"[3] yet we will find it is very difficult to break our Rule without committing some sin. For instance, in Chapter 2nd, Sec. 1st, the Rule says, "The Sisters appointed to attend the schools shall with all charity and humility, purity of intention, and confidence in God undertake the charge."[4] Therefore, if we labor in the schools to excite applause, to be noticed, or desire to be particularly noticed and distinguished in that office, by the children or others, this will be a breach of the Rule and a sin, for we should observe that it is only by performing those duties with the dispositions pointed out by the Rule that we will receive the glorious recompense promised to the faithful discharge of them.

By omitting through forgetfulness what is ordained in the 2nd section of the same chapter, we would not sin, unless we had been first desired by our Superior to make the offering, etc. We will, however, lose the assistance and grace we would assuredly have obtained had we done what is prescribed.[5] The Rule mentions particular matters and subjects on which the children are to be instructed, but it does not mean that each sister sent into the schools is to instruct them on these different subjects, but that they are to be given in the course of the different instructions.[6]

A sister may not "feel convinced that no work of charity can be more productive of good to society or more conducive to the happiness of the poor than the careful instruction of women."[7] She might think her services better employed in attending the dying, or in the House of Mercy.[8] Here is a breach of Rule without sin, although the Sister could and ought to bring her mind to the sentiments mentioned in the Rule. Remember, there is a great deal less said in the Rule on visiting the sick than on the manner of visiting them,[9] because it is this that makes the difference between worldlings and Religious. The former may be indulging their self-will, or their natural, generous, and benevolent dispositions, but the Religious should perform this duty in imitation of and for love of Jesus Christ, endeavouring to assimilate themselves more perfectly every day to Him, keeping His unwearied patience and humility constantly before their minds, thus encouraging themselves to act as He did, for it is only by doing so they will gain the crown of glory and title of Children of the Most High.

In visiting the sick, the sisters, when necessary, should acquaint them, with the greatest caution, that their recovery is hopeless. It would perhaps be better not to say to them they will not recover, fearing this abrupt announcement might create in them a feeling of dislike for the Sisters that could not be removed from their minds, and so prevent them deriving any benefit from the visit, or profiting by the instructions the sisters thought necessary to give. The sisters should, however, endeavor to make them see and know the danger they are in, and resign themselves to God's Holy Will.

The sisters should be very much on their guard with the young women in the House of Mercy, and should never ask them any questions relative to the situations they have left. All that is necessary to be known relative to them is that they have not forfeited their moral character, and this is enquired into by the sister appointed to that office.[10] We would expose ourselves to the danger of hearing many things improper for us to know did we listen to details and adventures. This is a matter of such importance that a Sister should not go to Communion without approaching the tribunal of Penance, after having through curiosity listened to their stories or made unnecessary enquiries from them on any subject. (What our Venerated Foundress says here of the caution and reserve to be observed with the young women in the House of Mercy can with great advantage be also applied to every extern that comes to the convent, whether tradesmen, workmen, adults for instruction, servants applying for situations, or even those engaged in the convent where there is no House of Mercy attached to it. All conversation with them should be avoided. No sister should enter into conversation with them or ask any questions except those appointed; otherwise we will be exposed to the danger mentioned by our Mother Foundress.) Sr. M. C. S. [or L. or D.][11]

We should have a most lively devotion to the Most Holy Sacrament of the Altar, often reflecting how dearly our Saviour purchased the happiness we enjoy and that which we hope to enjoy hereafter. He purchased it at the cost of His honor, dignity and life. If Jesus Christ were not present on the Altar, there would be no Convent. We would not like to live in it as we would be only like a number of persons congregated in any other house.[12]

The Rosary is a most powerful means of obtaining every other grace. If we do not obtain them, it is probable we do not say it as we ought. The "Holy Mary" in particular should be said with the greatest fervor, begging the Holy Virgin to assist us now and at the hour of our death.

There is nothing of greater consequence than the perfect discharge of our daily ordinary duties. Amongst them that of hearing Mass is the most important. From the moment the priest comes to the Altar, until he leaves it, we should endeavor to banish, with the greatest diligence, every thought that is not of God, and we ought to follow the priest through the different stages of the Holy Sacrifice by saying the short prayers used for that purpose, with the greatest diligence. A little before the Elevation we ought to beg of God to grant us for that day His enlivening, supporting, and animating grace. That will enable us to discharge all the duties of the day in such a manner as will give Him glory and sanctify our own souls. We should ask this with the same fervor as if we expected to die in half an hour after, and ask it but for one day only, for each day will bring a fresh supply for itself.

We should always endeavor to have a cheerful countenance and a manner equally free from constraint or levity. It is not necessary that the eyes be always cast down, for this might give to some a rather disagreeable expression of countenance, but the countenance should be always modest and ever pleasing to behold.

Nothing can be more disagreeable than to hear a Religious say anything *sharp* or *bitter.* It at once renders her habit and veil unbecoming to her. A professed sister is bound to try and prevent whatever she knows to be wrong, by charitably telling the faulty Sister to avoid such and such things; for instance, if she hears a sister disapprove of the domestic arrangements of the house, and speaking of the better arrangements of other houses, she ought to stop that conversation, but yet she should not become a censurer of her sister's actions, on every trifle, merely because she is professed.

A professed sister should be always ready to yield her opinion, particularly to the novices, and when it can be done without any compromise of duty, as the novices generally look up to the professed for example. There is a great difference between charity and mercy, for although Jesus Christ has done everything that charity could dictate, yet if His mercy is not exercised, after all how few will be saved!

Subjects proposed for Consideration during the Annual Retreats, Suitable for Retreat Sundays

1st Humility[13]

Humility is a virtue which makes us low and contemptible in our own eyes, and according to St. Bernard is twofold: 1st humility of the understanding, by which we know our own insufficiency, and 2nd of the will, by which we desire to be treated as the lowest.[14] See then, are you truly humble, not in words or appearance only, but in deed. It is not enough to have a clear knowledge of one's insufficiency and little worth; we must also entertain an habitual and serious contempt of ourselves, and be willing that everyone should despise us and treat us as we deserve.[15] If therefore you shun humiliations, if you feel hurt or annoyed when reminded of your faults, when your actions or exertions do not meet with the approbation you expected, or when you think the attention or respect due to your rank in religion is not given you, you are far from possessing this necessary and heavenly virtue. Therefore, you should make every effort during this retreat to acquire a sincere spirit of humility.

"It is a shame," says St. Bernard, "to wish to be honored in a religious house, which is the school of humility." But let your humility be unfeigned and more in your heart than in your words. Let it appear by your actions and by your whole conduct, that you really wish to be unnoticed, that you seek no esteem, no particular attention. Show yourself ready to yield to all and to serve and oblige everyone. "The greater thou art," says the author of the *Imitation,* "humble thyself the more in all things, and thou shalt find grace before God, and thou shalt have complied with the treaty of thy dear Master Who says, 'Learn of Me, for I am meek and humble of heart.'" "The greater thou art," that is, the purer and more holy thou art, either by preserving thy first innocence or by the guard you have over yourself, the more, by one thought of pride or vanity indulged, you would lose all.

The 3rd degree of humility is that to which Religious are bound by their holy state. It consists in preferring poverty, privations, and contempt because they were preferred by our Saviour. This preference should not originate in a natural, easy indifference which would make us say, "I do not care what I take or what is given me," but from solid virtue which, without feeling a disgust for the lawful enjoyments of life which God in His bounty has given to His creatures and permits them to enjoy, prompts us willingly to deprive ourselves of them, because He did so, and in order to resemble Him the more. So that if we feel inclined to find fault with anything that is given us, our food, clothes etc., our holy state obliges us to submit with patience to those little privations and even to rejoice in them because they make us more closely resemble our dear Redeemer. We may perceive from all our instructions that a strong and lively faith is the solid foundation of all virtues. We must often beg of God to grant us this faith, and to preserve us from the dreadful inconsistency of contradicting it and our Religious Profession by our actions.

2nd On the Evils of Pride

It is not enough to bewail sin in general; we must aim at its extirpation from the very root. Otherwise the soul would not be purified nor can she happily arrive at her last end. Now the root of all evil is pride. The Holy Scriptures positively declare it: "Pride is the beginning of all sin," and again "Never suffer pride to remain in thy mind or in thy words, for from it all perdition took its beginning." This vice is more to be dreaded than any other as it insinuates by apparently humble motives, and is oftentimes concealed under them.

Examine now if this vice has any place in your mind, in your words, in your actions. Do you wish to be praised or preferred to others? The holy Prophet Isaias says "that such are exceedingly proud." Do you love the 1st place and those employments which may rank you above others, and give you an occasion to exercise authority? Are you displeased that the less distinguished and lower offices (if any office in God's house can be termed low) are marked out for you? Do you feel jealousy or uneasiness at seeing others more esteemed than you? If so, the evil root still remains. If you do not now endeavor to pluck it up, it will be the cause of much injury to your soul; it will render you troublesome to those with whom you live, but much more so to yourself. It will keep you at a distance from God and deprive you of many graces, for

"God rejects the proud while He gives His grace to the humble."

We never can be happy, nor feel as we ought, until we bring ourselves to the consideration that we are treated better than we deserve. This is really the case, and it may be said of the purest and most holy amongst us, while with how much more justice of those who know their own unworthiness. If we keep this before our eyes, we will not be surprised that we are treated or spoken to in such and such a manner, but rather wonder that we meet with so much attention and are permitted to dwell under the same roof with so many more faithful spouses of Jesus Christ than ourselves.

3rd On Self-Denial

Not only penitents and Saints, but Religious too should study the useful lesson of self-denial. Why so afflicted when spoken to in a manner we fancy unkind? Why so displeased when reproved in the spirit of Charity? Because I want the true spirit of self-denial; and Christ says, "If anyone wishes to come after Me, let him deny himself, take up his Cross, and follow Me." How can I labor for the glory of God, for the salvation of those committed to my care, and my own perfection if I have not the spirit of self-denial? How can I practise angelic purity, profound humility, and entire resignation to the Divine Will in all things without this heavenly virtue? And am I not a stranger to it, without restraint in my interior or exterior, always prone to the indulgence of my senses and inclinations? How then can I call myself a disciple of Jesus Christ, Who says, "Whosoever does not take up his cross and follow Me, is not worthy of Me."

Let us now resolve to enter into this blessed, secure way of self-denial which infallibly leads to Heaven. Let us walk in the path which Jesus Christ Himself has marked out for us. He will assist our weakness and reward us a hundred fold for the most trifling acts of self-denial we perform for His sake. O my merciful Saviour! You know my weakness. Vouchsafe to assist me with Your powerful grace!

We seem to forget that God calls upon us to take up our cross, and that this cross must be composed of the sacrifice of something that is dear to us, that He requires of us constant watchfulness over our thoughts and words. Is this restraint, this self-denial to make us gloomy, sad or peevish? No, such is not His intention, for it is to the religious loaded with her cross that He has in particular promised the hundred fold, but then this is a conditional promise. It is not made to those who drag the cross after them, who almost push it from them. No, it is to those who take it up generously, courageously, and lovingly. To them He will make the bitter things sweet and the sweet things bitter. He will make mortification, self-denial, and penance sweet and delightful, and worldly enjoyments and the things they have left, bitter, so as to feel nothing for them but disgust.

We can never give Glory to God or serve our neighbour without practising this self-denial and mortification. A Religious ought to observe them in every way that is possible, so far as her health and strength will permit. How often do we go to a Sister to say, "we hope she did not think we meant so or so, on such an occasion," persuading ourselves we are actuated by charity, where it is only our self love that will not rest easy while there is an unfavorable opinion formed of us. We have removed ourselves from the cross which accompanies the vanities, cares, and solicitudes of worldlings, and we come to carry the cross of Jesus Christ, which is free from all those things. But do we not shake it off whenever it is possible? God would certainly assist us, did we labor earnestly to acquire these heavenly virtues, and reward us ten-fold for any little act we would practise of either. Both virtues are called heavenly because so free from all that is earthly and so opposite to our natural feelings and sentiments. We need only consider how dear our own will has been to us, from our earliest years, to know how acceptable a sacrifice it is to God. O my God, give us grace to be faithful in the practice of those virtues.

Mortification of the body may be compared to mortification of the spirit. Nothing is more painful or more keenly felt in the body than the former. So in the spirit, a mortification is something that wounds us, that touches us to the very heart. Yet if we bear patiently with and even love it for the love of God, after it we will enjoy true peace.

4th On the Predominant Passion

It is of the greatest importance to know the predominant passion; it is the foundation of the work of perfection. We should often beg of God, by fervent prayer, to make it known to us, for from our predominant passion unmortified (the fruitful source of all evil) proceeds the many faults we daily commit. We should examine whether it be pride, sloth, love of creatures, self love, etc.[16]

There is often as much passion and self opinion in desiring and requesting that what we do should not be noticed, nor our name mentioned, as there is pride in the contrary. We should endeavor to feel quite indifferent to all these things, and remember, whether we are noticed now or not, the time will come in a few years when we and our actions will be forgotten and unknown.

Let us then examine carefully if we have given our hearts entirely to God, how far and how long we have wandered from the end of our creation, and opposed the designs of God over us. How far we have departed from the command He gave us of loving Him with our whole heart and soul, and mind and strength. Would not a person unacquainted with the Gospel truths judge from our conduct heretofore the command was to love ourselves and creatures and to forget God? These considerations should humble us, and excite us to make the only return we can to God, by great exertions in the discharge of our duties.

5th On the Particular Examen[17]

The particular Examen is one of the most powerful helps in the spiritual life, as it is the most efficacious means of extirpating sin and practising virtue. We should take for the subject of our particular examen, first our predominant failing, as it is the greatest impediment to our perfection, the source of our daily faults, and which if not curbed and destroyed will certainly lead to sin.

We should also make our examen on the manner in which we perform our ordinary duties, on fervor in prayer, on recollection both interior and exterior, on purity of intention, but our chief care should be to acquire the virtue we stand in need of, and which is most opposed to our predominant defect. Rest on one point at a time, and do not hurry from one thing to another. See now how you have hitherto attended to this most necessary and important duty, and resolve to perform it for the future with the great[est] exactness. It is a useful practice to set down the number of faults you notice at each examen, and to perform some acts of self-denial in atonement for them. This is a duty no one can perform for you, neither bishop, priest, nor superior. They cannot take your mind into theirs and say, "I will settle this matter for you." They can only point out the means.

The same faults frequently committed cease to be imperfections; they become sins. This is compared in Scriptures to the most loathsome thing that can possibly be, casting them out of our souls by Confession, and returning to them again, "Like a dog to his vomit."

6th On the Performance of our ordinary Duties

To perform our actions as we ought, constant and perpetual self-denial is necessary. The circumstance of David pouring out the water that was brought to him when he felt great thirst would not have been recorded in the Scriptures if not an action acceptable to God. We may learn from this how pleasing in the sight of Heaven is the least act of self-denial, even leaving the least thing at meals, which could not possibly injure the health.[18]

Our most important actions are those which relate to God, and upon the manner in which we discharge these our progress in perfection principally depends. The 2nd class of duties relate to our neighbour. We must edify all, by modesty, sweetness, and evenness of temper. The modesty here spoken of has particular reference to the manner of expressing ourselves, avoiding all strong expressions or being too decided in giving an opinion. Above all, we should endeavor to preserve evenness of temper, and though it is not possible we can always feel the same calm state of mind, yet we should be on our guard that any crosses or sorrows do not appear on our countenance or manner.[19]

The 3rd class of duties relate to ourselves. They appear trifling, but when done through a motive of virtue are seeds of eternal life, and there is not one of them that Almighty God will not take into account: Rising, dressing, meals, Recreation, walk, tone of voice, cleanliness, gentleness, etc., etc.

Rising the moment we are called, and begging of God, if He spare us for that one day, we may spend it in such a manner as may be meritorious of eternal life.

Endeavoring while dressing to keep our minds recollected, and at all times dressing quickly. This is one of the few duties that ought to be performed in haste. We ought also pay great attention to our appearance, with the pure intention of pleasing God.

Meals—not to eat or drink with eagerness, nor to pass any observation on the sisters, as to whether they eat heartily or not, or what they take.

Conversation—to avoid bringing ourselves into notice, either directly or indirectly; sometimes to refrain from saying what would be innocent, in a spirit of mortification, making an offering of it to God.

Watching our manner and countenance, that both may be always pleasing, and never gloomy or harsh, although at the same time we may be sorrowful. It is said of our Redeemer that He was always pleasing to behold, and never sad or troublesome.[20]

All our actions must be performed with exactness, fervor, and perseverance.[21]

1st. Exactness, not the exactness with which people in the world perform their actions, who are naturally precise and like regularity, and who give way to impatience and peevishness when put out of their way, but with that exactness which makes us observe the time and place appointed, because we are doing it for the love of God, and through obedience.

2nd. Fervor may be exercised in the midst of disgusts and aridities, and although we may feel a great disrelish for prayer, and almost feel glad when it is over, yet if we go to it with a determined resolution of not letting ourselves be carried away by temptation, we may be said to be truly fervent. We must then say, "My God, I am satisfied to remain in Thy Presence as Thou pleasest; if Thou sendest me consolation, I shall feel grateful; if not, I am satisfied." We should also, when performing our actions for God, act as we would for a person we tenderly loved, saying in our hearts and minds, "I will do this very well, I will take great pains with it, because it will please God whom I love, who views me, and who is to be my Judge and my reward."

3rd. Perseverance—Perseverance is a constant exercise of self-denial, and serves to keep the body in subjection to the spirit. Thus each day will bring us nearer to that perfection to which we are bound to aspire; thus the saints acquired so high a degree of sanctity.

7th On the Graces annexed to the Religious State

External graces consist in prayer, lectures, Sacraments, etc., etc. Woe be to those in whom they produce no effect, no solid virtue.[22]

We call that virtue solid which is our own, and which, with God's assistance, depends on ourselves and not on others or on circumstances which are continually liable to change. See if our virtue depend on the tone of voice, the words or manners of another; then it is [on] their good qualities and not on our own virtue we are depending.[23]

We ought often reflect on the manner in which the Blessed Virgin replied to the Angel when he announced to her the mystery of the Incarnation. She did not say one unnecessary word or ask a single unnecessary question. What a lesson to us to refrain from making unnecessary enquiries which have their source in mere curiosity. We should implore her assistance in visiting the sick and beg grace to perform that action with the same charity, prudence, reserve, and modesty with which she would have performed it were she on earth.

The longer we are in religion, the more humble, patient, and subdued our manners ought to become. They ought to be free from all hurry, agitation, and discomposure, our language simple and free from all strong terms. What a shame should we bring the practices of religion into disrepute by remaining in imperfections, and leaving it in the power of younger sisters to say, "Of what use are retreats and religious observances when such a sister remains the same after them."

Our Saviour lying in the tomb is an exact representation of what a religious ought to be. The life of seclusion is represented by His enclosure in the monument, her obedience by His remaining there till the time appointed by His Father for His Resurrection, but above all, her union with God by His union with His Father.

8th On the Love of God

Since Charity is the Queen of all virtues, the enemy constantly endeavors to deprive us of it. It is therefore necessary that we should be on our guard lest we be deceived, and think we possess that virtue when we scarcely know what it is.

The 1st mark of one's being animated by this holy love is not to be attached to ourselves or to any created object except in the manner ordained by God. Wherefore, take the determination of Abraham, and at once sacrifice to God the chains that bind you. A victory over self-love is a sure sign that divine love is cherished by us.

The 2nd mark is to do and suffer cheerfully whatever we know to be pleasing to God. Examine then with what fidelity you embrace the opportunity of doing something for the love of our Creator. What have you endured for His Sake? Are you watchful not to lose any occasion of practising virtue, especially meekness and humility, so necessary and so dear to the Heart of Our Saviour?

The 3rd mark is a strict conformity of our will with the Holy Will of God. See if you really perform what obedience prescribes, or what God demands of you. Do you faithfully comply with His Holy inspirations? In time of pain and affliction are these your words: "The Lord gave and the Lord hath taken away. Blessed be His Name forever," also "Not my will, Oh Lord, but Thine be done"? Do you always study and practise with delight this lesson of your Divine Redeemer: "Love one another as I have loved you," which is so necessary to preserve peace and union, that God may behold in all but one heart and one soul. Look at Christ dead on the Cross. Behold how He loved you. Can you refuse to love Him or to do what He asks of you? Lord Jesus, implant Your love in my heart. It is all I desire in this world or in the next! We must be on our guard against the temptation that would make us think that things were said or thought of us that never entered anyone's head, and thus excite in us some uncharitable feelings against others.

The manner in which we are to be attached to created objects as Religious is very different from the way in which people in the world may be attached to them. As to our parents, relations, and friends, we can no longer enter into their worldly concerns or projects with interest, or question them on them. If we do, we go to the world we have left. We are worldlings under the religious habit. They cannot enter our world, we cannot enter theirs, without being unfaithful.

We may imagine with what displeasure Jesus Christ looks down upon the religious who entertains her visitors with the affairs of the convent, who communicates to them her trials and difficulties, who listens with eagerness to their worldly views. "Ah, faithless spouse," He will say, "is it thus you act, you whom I called away from the world, you whom I separated from its dangers. You are My Spouse only in appearance." This worldlings themselves seem to understand for they will tell you: "If she were settled in the farthest part of the world, we might communicate every little thing to each other, but now that she is in the convent, it is quite a different separation, for it is a death to all she left in the world. She will be dead even to me." Woe be to the Religious who removes this first impression from their minds, with which it would seem God Himself inspired them to teach all what the Religious state really is.

Let us examine further and see how we stand on this point of true charity, or the love of God. Are we willing on all occasions to die to ourselves, or are we not feelingly alive to all that concerns self or interferes in the least with our happiness? Are we willing to perform whatever is imposed on us by obedience, be it ever so opposed to nature's feelings, assured that however unworthy the person appointed to direct be, God will not fail to enlighten her and give her the necessary graces, since the happiness of His dear children is therein concerned.

We offer to God our feet and hands, our talents, etc., but if we wish to offer Him our hearts (and it is this He requires) we should have [them] mortified and humble. Do we offer them generously to God, or do we not rather shelter them from all that might afflict them? In vain can we hope to be united to God in any other way than by the cross. The exercises of charity in which any generous heart takes pleasure will not affect this union. The heart must be crucified, before it can be closely united to the Heart of a Crucified Saviour. Sweet Jesus, grant me Thy love. It is that I ask in time or eternity.

9th On Good Purposes

Good purposes are the result of serious reflections grounded on faith and made in the presence of God. The attention should be fixed on the acquisition of solid virtue, not that devotion which consists in saying many prayers, in sighing and being often on our knees. Our object must be to correct whatever is defective in our religious or moral conduct. [24] When we speak of the morality of the Gospel, we mean that if we, religious, were performing a duty in a slothful, careless manner, we would be acting contrary to the morality which says "He that contemneth small things shall fall by little and little."

The 1st fruit we should draw from good resolutions is a solid hatred of sin, that is, through love of God to refrain from saying, or doing, or thinking anything we know to be displeasing to Him. For instance, I will not say this vain or mortifying word, I will not dwell on this uncharitable thought, I will not entertain this jealous or angry feeling, because it will be displeasing to God. We should examine the manner in which we perform our actions, and pay particular attention to those duties in which we have experienced most sloth and weariness. When we fail, we should perform some little penance lest we lose some of the grace given us at this precious time.

We must not, however, be discouraged at our own imperfections, for it is as displeasing to God to be guilty of impatience towards ourselves as to be guilty of it towards others. We must avoid saying to ourselves, "Oh, why did I say so and so? I did not think I could act so," but humbly, meekly, and quietly have recourse to God. Nothing can be well done or give glory to Him in which we give way to inquietude, for He has declared that He would not dwell in a troubled heart. We should carefully avoid yielding to those feelings which betray weakness of character. A Religious is a person in whom everything should be tranquil and subdued, and from whom everything childish and trifling should be banished. In making resolutions, we should avoid determining to say long prayers, of [or] being more frequently in the choir, or anything tending to excite scruple.

Nothing will promote our advancement in perfection more

than charity, or draw down greater blessings on us than strict attention to every branch of it. One prayer from a well regulated, charitable heart and mind will have more weight with God than hours of prayer from one who neglects these points.

If we are humble and sincere, God will finish in us the work He has begun. He never refuses His grace to those who ask it. Let us not feel distressed that others know our faults, we all have imperfections and will have them to our death. God has never bestowed all His choicest blessings on one person. He did not give to St. Peter what He gave to St. Paul, nor to either what He gave to St. John.

10th On Forming good Resolutions from each Meditation

A meditation without a firm resolution is like a body without a soul, and even the resolution without the requisite dispositions or conditions is a light without heat. We should be watchful never to fail in this most important point of meditation. Indeed, without it our meditations will be unprofitable and may lead us into great illusions. With regard to the resolution, it should be confined to one particular matter, whether the thing is to be done or omitted. We should see how this is to be effected and select means for that end. 2nd. We should reduce our resolutions to practice on the day of meditation. This will be greatly facilitated by calling to mind during the day the reflections which made most impression on us in the morning meditation. This will also promote union with God, which is the essence of Religious life. Is it thus you perform your meditation? Do you go to it with a firm intention of profiting by it, and drawing from it motives for the correction of your faults and the practice of every virtue? "Confiding in your mercy and goodness, Oh God, I presume to ask that I may hereafter make meditation in the manner most pleasing to you, as by doing so I shall obtain the most efficacious means of becoming a perfect Religious."

11th On Indifference to any Office in God's House

God being my last end, I should in this Retreat make a firm purpose to serve Him in that perfect state and office to which I am called. For this I should have an entire indifference to whatever is appointed for me by obedience, anxious only that His blessed Will may be done in my regard. But am I thus disposed? or is there anything prevents me attaining the perfection in God's service to which I am bound to aspire? What are my secret wishes? I should dread the evil of self-will, which St. Bernard says is the sole cause of hell.[25]

Be then ever like the angels, prompt to obey the voice of God, equally fervent in the discharge of every duty marked out for you, always bearing in mind that you are a Christian and a Religious and as such you should especially belong to God. Remember that hereafter you are to serve Him with greater diligence in everything, even the smallest office relating to your charge. "Grant, Oh my God, I may now begin, for all that I have hitherto done is nothing."

"If there were no self-will, there would be no hell." Does it not seem that God, in drawing us to a state in which we are freed from this tyrant and placed under obedience, wished in a particular manner to shield us from so great a danger as that of hell, placing us in a sort of happy necessity of being freed from its baneful influence.

12th On the good use of Time

There is nothing ought to fill us with greater remorse than reflection on the time we have misspent, or spent uselessly and unprofitably, as all that time should be considered as lost in which we have not been employed either for the glory of God or our own sanctification.[26] We should be delighted now at having every moment of time filled up by duties that obedience imposes on us, as thus we will have less time at our own disposal and less to account for. Should any time remain, we must carefully avoid spending it in idle conversation. How can we expect to be recollected in prayer if we be habitually dissipated? Perhaps the time we wasted was that in which God was ready to give us the greatest lights and graces, had we been attentive and faithful to Him.

Each day is a step which we take towards Eternity, and we will continue to step thus from day to day until we take the last, which will bring us into the Presence of God. We cannot now afford to lose any more time. What remains is too short to prepare for that Heavenly Country to which we are journeying.

13th On Recollection

All Christians are bound to love God, but especially Religious, and because they are the special objects of His choice, He has withdrawn them from whatever might render this difficult. The least, therefore, they can do is to endeavor to cooperate with His merciful designs in drawing them to this holy state, which is to be united to Himself.

A good use of mental prayer and a great love of the hidden life will be necessary to effect this. We should be delighted to be unknown that we might the more resemble our divine Saviour who was always occupied and constantly doing a great deal, without bringing Himself into notice or being distinguished. Do we love silence? or do we regret the arrival of the time prescribed for it? Why should we regret? It is the time in which the soul will most advance towards God. Do we speak too fast or too much? If so, we will not be recollected. Religious gravity is most beautiful, most attractive, but it is quite different, quite opposed to gloom or sullenness. It repels all intrusion and renders familiarity impossible. Whatever is done without having God in view is either sinful or unprofitable. Every thought, word, and action that is infected with the poison of self love and self-gratification is a fraud on the rights of God.

As no time is so favorable for establishing the love of God in the heart as retreat, we should be most earnest in the search. There are two means by which it is chiefly obtained: Recollection of mind and the constant study of prayer. Recollection is an habitual exercise of the understanding and will by which the soul, as it were, lives in God. To obtain recollection, we must entertain a great love of silence. "In silence and in quiet the devout soul becomes familiar with God." Examine now how you observe silence. Are you silent in the times and places marked out? In speaking, do you avoid useless and unprofitable conversation, which never can promote piety or the union of your soul with God? See also what is your manner of speaking. Is it loud or hasty, or does your whole manner bespeak the Religious?

It is vain to think of keeping our minds recollected if we do not practise religious gravity and reserve. Do you attend to the Presence of God, frequently remembering that He beholds you, and uniting yourself to Him by ardent affections? Do you apply to prayer? Do you attend to the distant and immediate preparation for it? Do you feel a love for this holy exercise, and do you employ every means to render it profitable?

To obtain a great love for God has been the object of the retreat. If this was not effected, it was all so much time lost. Nothing will facilitate this more than ardent aspirations of divine love in the secret of the heart. We cannot fall into excess in this intercourse between God and our hearts. We may address Him as a dear Friend, to Whom we owe a great deal, saying, "What would I do only for You? What can I give You in return? I owe You everything." If this became a habit, it would soon produce recollection and be the best distant preparation we could make for prayer. It would also keep us continually in the Presence of God.

[The compiled manuscript of Catherine McAuley's oral instructions ends here.]

Editor's Note

In the compiled manuscript, this chapter is labeled "Chapter 6th," but it immediately follows "Chapter 4th."

The main *archetypes* for chapter 5 that have so far been discovered are four: the Bermondsey manuscript numbered IOLM/BER/12/1/4, and the Liverpool manuscript numbered IOLM/LIV/1/1, both of which are preserved in AIMGB and whose probable provenance is discussed in the Editor's Note to chapter 1; several parts of the small 168-page leather-bound manuscript book (4 inches x 7 inches), which is numbered CMA/1/5/2, written in several different hands, and preserved in the Baggot Street collection at MCA (Catherine McAuley's printed manuscript is contained in this notebook and is discussed in the Editor's Note to chapter 2); and Mary Gonzaga O'Brien's notebook in the New Hampshire (U.S.A.) collection now preserved in MHCSMA in Belmont, North Carolina.

Mary Gonzaga O'Brien entered the Sisters of Mercy in Providence, Rhode Island; accompanied Frances Warde to Manchester, New Hampshire in 1858; served for a time in Bangor, Maine; and then returned to Manchester. She was present at Frances Warde's death on September 23, 1884, and then succeeded her as reverend mother. For about thirty years, she was not only Frances Warde's assistant, but also her closest friend. It is therefore reasonable to assume that Frances shared with Mary Gonzaga her knowledge of Catherine McAuley's oral teachings as well as any manuscripts of Catherine's instructions that Frances had carried with her from Ireland to Pittsburgh in 1843 and finally to Manchester. Mary Gonzaga O'Brien's notebook contains many prayers, maxims, and other personal spiritual texts; but it also contains toward the end many pages of instructions that match the content and wording of much of chapter 5. In these pages of her notebook, Mary Gonzaga may have been transcribing a manuscript that was in Mary Frances Warde's own hand. If so, no such Warde manuscript has so far been discovered.

A primary and obvious *source* for much of chapter 5 is Louis Bourdaloue's *Spiritual Retreat for Religious Persons* (1828 English edition). Other probable *sources* for the wording or content in parts of this chapter are Rodriguez, *Practice,* vols. 1 and 2, and Baudrand, *Soul on Calvary.* Where these dependences occur, further notes are given.

Part 3

The Present-Day Relevance of Catherine McAuley's Instructions

The Letter to the Hebrews urges us to remember that "here we have no lasting city, but we are looking for the city that is to come" (13:14), and the author of Revelation prophesies:

> I saw a new heaven and a new earth, for the first heaven and the first earth had passed away, and the sea was no more. And I saw the holy city, the new Jerusalem, coming down out of heaven from God.... And I heard a loud voice from the throne saying, "See, the home of God is among mortals. He will dwell with them as their God, and they will be his peoples, and God himself will be with them; he will wipe every tear from their eyes...." I saw no temple in the city, for its temple is the Lord God the Almighty, and the Lamb. (21:1–4, 22)

Catherine McAuley clung in hope to this promise of the full reign of God. Substituting the metaphor of one's "own country" for the "holy city" coming from God, she counseled that every Sister of Mercy, and indeed every human person, "should consider herself... a stranger and a pilgrim on earth, having her conversation in Heaven ... as every day she is preparing to enter into her own country" (38–39).[1] Like Pope Francis, she believed that the church "is first and foremost a people advancing on its pilgrim way towards God," drawn forward by "the free and gracious initiative of God."[2]

In her oral instructions, she reminds us that "in creating the world" God "only intended it as a place of pilgrimage, but in Heaven," that is, in the full reign of God, "is combined all that His infinite power, goodness, and love could effect to conduce to your happiness. Behold a place … waiting there for you" (105). Here Catherine does not mean, and Jesus Christ never meant, that the world and its peoples' historical needs and conditions are to be disregarded as simply the ever-changing backdrop or scenery along the route of our pilgrim journey. The whole mystery and history of God's self-communication in the incarnation of Jesus the Christ says the opposite of that. "As you have sent me into the world, so I have sent them into the world" (John 17:18). The sending into history of Jesus, and of his disciples, implies a mission there, and a "coming back" when the mission is consummated.

Christians, as followers of Christ, the Savior of the world, are to be "the light of the world," hope-carrying, prophetic presences and actors in the world, shining lamps along the pilgrim way, giving "light to all in the house" (Matt. 5:14–15) through mercifully loving one another "as I have loved you" (John 15:12). But since we "do not belong to the world," we are not to settle down in it spiritually, for the reign of God, the kingdom of Christ—though it "has come near you" (Luke 10:9)—"is not from this world" (John 18:26). As Nicholas Lash puts it in *Theology for Pilgrims,* "we are people on the way, on pilgrimage, a people whose finishing began at Calvary and at the empty tomb, but which lies ahead of us in the consummation of the kingdom."[3]

One of the difficulties of the Christian life is our static but understandable attachment to *this* human life, *this* world, and our seeming inability, if left to ourselves, to grasp in dynamic hope the reality of the life to come, into which will be gathered all created life and history, including our own. As St. Bernard put it, we confuse our "exile" with our true "homeland."[4] Only the accompanying love of God can turn our dim eyes toward "what no eye has seen, nor ear heard, nor the human heart conceived, what God has prepared for those who love him" (1 Cor. 2:9). Meanwhile, "faith, hope, and love abide, these three; and the greatest of these is love" (1 Cor. 13:13).

We are "pilgrims" on this earth—on foot together, during this "little while that we call the history of the world."[5] This is the quintessential message of Catherine's oral instructions to the first Sisters of Mercy and to the whole church: "Each day is a step which we take towards Eternity, and we will continue to step thus from day to day until we take the last, which will bring us into the Presence of God. We cannot now afford to lose any more time. What remains is too short to prepare for the Heavenly Country to which we are journeying" (154).

In no way did Catherine see herself as a leader of our human pilgrimage, but simply as a companion on our common journeying, a soul-friend who lifts a shining lamp and suggests some helpful "steps" along the way. Her instructions are some of those steps, shared as reverently and humbly as when she and the first Mercy sisters visited the sick and dying poor in their Dublin hovels, "preserving recollection of mind and going forward as if they expected to meet their Divine Redeemer in each poor habitation."[6]

Although Catherine's suggestions about the vows that religious profess will be most helpful to members of religious orders and congregations, the evangelical life which those vows hope to serve and embody is also the call of the Gospel to all Christians. Vowed religious life is simply a deliberate, public promise to try—as best one humanly can with God's help—to live that Gospel call and the life-encompassing meaning of baptism into Christ's life, death, and resurrection. Catherine's focus on the "Way" Jesus announces (John 14:6) is the reason why so much of what she says is of enduring value not only to her Mercy family and other women and men religious living in the twenty-first century, but also to theologians, spiritual writers and directors, and indeed to all who wish to live deeply Christian lives. Her words as well as her life can be for all a shining lamp giving light along the Way.

Since we are now reasonably confident that the compiled manuscript of Catherine McAuley's oral instructions, as presented in this volume, is an authentic rendering, insofar as humanly possible, of some of what she actually said to her first companions, what did she say? What topics did she apparently most wish to highlight?

The "steps" Catherine explicitly offers in her oral instructions to her companion pilgrims, then as well as now, seem to cluster around four main themes of the Gospel:

1. our call to resemble Jesus Christ—his spirit, his faith, his example, his manner;
2. the primacy of universal "union and charity"—to the exclusion of all coldness, stiffness, and exceptions;
3. the willingness to embrace, peacefully and cheerfully, the portions of the cross of Christ that come to us, confident of the accompanying providence of God; and
4. the need for true humility of mind and heart as we stand before God and travel with our neighbors.

Those who are familiar with the life of Catherine McAuley and her purposes in founding the Sisters of Mercy may be surprised not to find in this list or in the text of her oral instructions (except three pages in chapter 5) many overt references to the works of mercy that were the fundamental reason for her life's work and for her creation of the Sisters of Mercy. Here, it may be helpful to understand that everything Catherine says in her oral instructions to the first Sisters of Mercy is intended to describe not so much their daily ministry about which she can assume they are well aware, but the Christlike spirit that should characterize their personal engagement in these works of mercy.

In the opening paragraph of the Rule and Constitutions she composed for the congregation, Catherine says, "what is peculiarly characteristic of this Institute of the Sisters of Mercy [is] a most serious application to the instruction of poor Girls, Visitation of the sick, and protection of distressed women of good character."[7] Even in Catherine's day these works of mercy, while always including a special concern for poor girls and women, were broadly interpreted to include all the human sufferings mentioned in Matthew's apocalyptic account of the Last Judgment; Catherine frequently quoted the words "Truly I tell you, just as you did it to one of the least of these who are members of my family, you did it to me" (Matt. 25:40). Like Jesus, she and her sisters always felt a special commitment to search out and serve the so-called least of God's people. Their merciful work in relation to those who were poor, sick, and/or debilitatingly ignorant in any way was, therefore, taken for granted in all Catherine's instructions to her sisters, whether written or oral, though it was sometimes more explicit in her written expressions. By the time the Rule was confirmed in Rome in 1841, the "service of the poor, the sick, and the ignorant" was so widely regarded as central to the raison d'être of the Sisters of Mercy that Catherine explicitly included this language as the fourth vow in their religious profession.

Certain words that are usually general in their meaning always stand in Catherine's oral instructions for the works of mercy. For example, when she uses the word "duties" or "labors" or "actions," as she frequently does, she is referring not only to inside-the-convent activities, but to the full range of spiritual and corporal works of mercy in which she and the community are engaged. Her references to "the law," "his service," even to "perfection" and "imitating" Jesus' life, also apply to the performance of these works of mercy, which, as she says, "constitute the business of our lives."[8]

However, in her oral instructions as in part 2, Catherine seems particularly eager to explain to her companions that *doing* the works of mercy will bear the fruit Jesus desires if it is animated by the *spirit* of the Gospel, if it is suffused by the interior spirit of the beatitudes and is imbued with the manner and attitudes Jesus himself displays and teaches. Therefore in these oral instructions she focuses on resemblance to Jesus, charity, patient suffering, and humility of heart, all the while assuming and implicitly connecting this evangelic spirit to the demanding works of mercy in which she knows her hearers are daily and deliberately engaged: the poor school and the shelter for homeless women at Baggot Street and the daily visitation of the sick and dying poor in their hovels and in hospitals.

Thus, in her oral instructions presented in part 2 of this volume, Catherine was primarily concerned about interior union with God and certain inner virtues that flow from that union. She believed that inner virtue, if it is real, will manifest itself exteriorly in our deeds and manner. It is hidden, but will reveal itself in the way we live and act. She also took for granted that we all have our defects and imperfections and "shall have them till our death." As she said, "God has never bestowed all His blessings on one person. He did not give to St. Peter what He gave to St. Paul, nor to either what He gave to St. John."[9] Yet she was convinced that God "never refuses His grace to those who ask it." So basically her instructions are about asking for God's help and then trying to live according to our request.

1. Central to Catherine's oral instructions is our need to grow in resemblance to Jesus Christ: resemblance to his spirit, his example, his virtue, and his manner. For her, the word "resemblance" seems to embrace much of what the New Testament tells us about "following" Christ. She says:

> The life and maxims of Jesus Christ should be as a book always open before us, in which we are to learn all that is necessary to know; as a glass in which we will clearly see our defects; and as a seal whose image we are to impress on our hearts. If we do not form our minds on the maxims of Jesus Christ, we will never acquire His evangelic spirit. (79)

She says of this resemblance:

> As little infants you must be born anew till Jesus Christ is formed in you. To have Jesus Christ formed in us is to think as He did, to speak as He spoke, and will as He willed. We must divest ourselves of all opinions, sentiments and judgments ... which are not conformable to His Spirit. This ... cannot be attained without difficulty and labor, but to it we are bound to aspire ... believing that Jesus Christ can and will effect this new birth within us, if we on our part do what He requires. (67–68)

Catherine frequently says that although one "should [happen to] possess talents, accomplishments, and everything that could make her amiable and admired, yet they would be of no value ... in the sight of God if she possessed not the spirit of Jesus Christ. She should pray most earnestly to Almighty God to bestow that spirit upon her" (91).

For Catherine, the spirit of Jesus Christ is revealed in the virtues and decisions of his human life:

His meekness ever the same under all circumstances.... His charity ever seeking some plea ... comforting the afflicted, healing the sick, showing the greatest tenderness for them, and evincing as much anxiety for their relief as if His own happiness depended on theirs. His patience under the severest pains of body and mind ... His sincerity and love of truth.... In like manner did He practice all the virtues; and this not for any short space of time, but at all times and in the most uniform and undeviating way. (78)

Catherine knows full well that none of us can ever perfectly resemble Jesus' virtues. We can only take to heart his plea: "Come to me ... and learn from me," and then try, as best we can, to follow his way. Therefore she says:

Let us take each of [Jesus'] virtues separately and meditate on the manner in which He practised them, and not leave off until we have succeeded in imitating Him as well as we can in each. Jesus Christ does not intend we should be as perfect as He, when He says, "Be ye perfect as also your heavenly Father is perfect." In order to follow this advice of our Saviour we should endeavor to do each action as perfectly as possible.... It is only by imitating the virtues of our Divine Master that His designs in our regard can be fulfilled. (93)

We can summarize Catherine's remarks about "resembling Jesus Christ" by recalling her *Practical Sayings,* as compiled by Mary Clare Moore. There Catherine says, "Be always striving to make yourselves like our blessed Lord; endeavor to resemble Him in some one thing at least, so that any person who sees you or speaks with you may be reminded of His sacred life on earth."[10] To hope to be, in some small way, a reminder of Jesus Christ "in some one thing at least" is a very humble desire and intention.

2. Catherine devotes many of her oral instructions to charity toward our neighbor, expanding on the chapters on "Union and Charity" and on the works of mercy in the Rule she com-

posed. Her comments are down-to-earth: she focuses on what true neighborly love looks like and sounds like. Her words are not simply idealistic, but deal with the nitty-gritty of human relations and genuine mercifulness. For her, universal charity is essential in any human life that hopes to be a following of Jesus Christ's life and words. As she says, "Where it reigns, every virtue flourishes.... Where it dwells, God also dwells; where *it does not exist, God cannot be.* The sister who does not practice this charity undermines as far as in her power our Institute, whilst the sweet, meek, charitable sister ... draws [God's] blessings on the Convent in which she dwells" (128). Catherine would say the same of the Church and of anyone who hopes to be "Christian."

The hardest lesson any of us ever learns is charity toward our neighbor—full-time, under-all-circumstances love of one another, not just "out on the streets," but at home. In her instructions Catherine goes so far as to claim that "our exercises of charity performed abroad will have no value before God if there be not established at home a solid foundation of this virtue, for the Scriptures tell us that 'well-regulated charity begins at home,' and it is on these conditions that our exterior duties will be acceptable to Him" (58). Catherine thus places love for one another, which she calls Jesus' "dying injunction," at the heart of the Institute of the Sisters of Mercy because "the one who loves another has fulfilled the law" (Rom. 13:8). She says, "If the love of God really reigns in your heart, it will quickly show itself in the exterior. You will become sweet and attractive in your manner. You will have a tender esteem for your Sisters and for everyone, beholding in them the image of God" (124).

As one reads Catherine's instructions on universal charity, one realizes that she is dead-set against pompousness, harshness, coldness, stiffness, and exceptions in our relations with our neighbors. She tells us to take care "not to act like a mistress in the world" when our directions are not attended to. She speaks of "cordial affection" for everyone, which "consists not in the outward appearance, but in a true, sincere, and heartfelt affection for all, not [just for] such or such a one because she happens to be more spiritual, or has more pleasing manners than another. For this would not be loving them as Christ loves us, nor be following the example He has given us, who when Judas approached to betray Him called him by the tender name of friend" (57).

"Cordial" is a central word in Catherine's understanding of charity. Clare Moore says that she frequently used to say, "Our mutual respect and charity is to be 'cordial'—now 'cordial' signifies something that revives, invigorates, and warms; such should be the effects of our love for each other."[11] A sentence for a refrigerator door if there ever was one!

What is difficult for us is the concrete daily practice of such universal love — the self-denial it requires, the silence, the listening, the biting of one's tongue, the "letting things pass," the seeing from another's point of view, the reaching out, the generosity, the self-bestowal, the renunciations of self-love. Here Catherine asks her hearers to turn to the example of God:

> When God finds a soul … acting with coldness and want of affection, He does not say He cannot act towards her as He formerly did, and that He must withdraw His grace from her, no, but His greatest care is to make her return to Him.… How strongly should this example excite all to union and charity if there be any difficulty in the practice, as there certainly may be, when we meet with coldness and reserve for our kindness and affection. (58–59)

To those of us who simply like to talk or write about union and charity, Catherine says plainly, in her direct and penetrating way, "It is much safer … to practice virtue, than to admire it by words ... however elegant and attractive." "Let us not love in word nor in tongue, but in deed and in truth," for "the proof of love is deeds." "If we love God, we will undoubtedly love our neighbour also; they are as cause and effect.... As it is impossible to love God without manifesting a love for our neighbour, so it is equally impossible to love our neighbour without manifesting it in our conduct" (125–26).

Catherine summarizes her thoughts on charity in this straightforward remark:

> Even our greatest ingratitude does not cool [Jesus Christ's] love for us.... Hence, if we indulge any coldness or pique towards our sisters [or others], though we were to perform the most heroic deeds of charity towards our neighbour, though the city were in admiration of our works, our charity will be imperfect, wanting what is essential to render our works pleasing to God, that is, charity of the mind and heart. Without this our labors will be as froth before God. (127)

3. A third theme in Catherine's instructions—one she relates to cheerfulness—is our need to carry, not "drag," the portions of the cross of Christ that are offered to us. As she says:

> We seem to forget that God calls upon us to take up our cross, and that this cross must be composed of the sacrifice of something that is dear to us; that He requires of us constant watchfulness over our thoughts and words. Is this ... self-denial to make us gloomy, sad or peevish? No, such is not His intention, for it is to the [one] loaded with her cross that He has in particular promised the hundred fold, but then this is a conditional promise. It is not made to those who drag the cross after them, who almost push it from them. No, it is to those who take it up generously, courageously, and lovingly. To them He will make the bitter things sweet and the sweet things bitter. (142)

Catherine knew her own share of "portions of the Cross of Christ," as she called them; they came to her just as she believed they had come to Jesus Christ: as a consequence of fidelity to her mission of Mercy, the spiritual and corporal works of mercy, and to what she took to be God's will for her. She did not go looking for crosses to carry. She does not advocate dolorism: the glorification of suffering for its own sake. Rather she urges us to embrace peacefully and cheerfully the "crosses," large and small, that come to us unbidden: the behavior and misunderstandings of others, their unwarranted criticisms, our own illnesses and personal losses, the arrangements we don't like, and even our own failures.

Catherine herself experienced all these portions of the Cross of Christ: for instance, in the inconvenience of another sister's frequent moodiness and frets; in the need to defend the sacramental rights of the women sheltered in the House of Mercy against the parish priest's neglect of them; in the public humiliation of the lawsuit and eviction from Kingstown when, having requested that the parish build schoolrooms for the poor girls she saw loitering about the roads, she then could not pay the building debt wrongfully ascribed to her; and in the burden of her own lack of patience. While she does not advocate rigid austerities or mortifications that will injure one's health, she does urge tranquil acceptance of the occasions for self-denial and cross-carrying that crop up in the normal course of life.

Catherine recognized that some portions of the cross of Christ offered to Christians are large and heavy, and that these can be carried only with Christ's help and trust in the perhaps hidden, but unfailing, accompaniment of God. She also recognized that many smaller so-called crosses are made worse—for ourselves and others—by our dragging them, our muttering about them, our peevishness, or as she says, by our "making much about nothing, attaching importance to the most trifling things" (89).

For her, the difference between cross-carrying and cross-dragging is interior; it lies in self-denial and in unhesitating confidence in the providence of God:

> Not only penitents and Saints, but [we] too should study the useful lesson of self-denial.... How can I labor for the glory of God, for the salvation of those committed to my care ... if I have not the spirit of self-denial? How can I practice ... entire resignation to the Divine Will in all things without this heavenly virtue? ... How then can I call myself a disciple of Jesus Christ Who says, "Whosoever does not take up his cross and follow Me, is not worthy of Me." (141)

Thus, for Catherine, our willingness to carry the portions of the Cross of Christ that come to us will be related to the strength of our desire to resemble and follow Jesus Christ. As she says:

> The life of Jesus Christ on which we are to model ourselves was a life of continual self-denial and sufferings.... His sufferings never caused Him to be sad or gloomy. His countenance was at all times delightful to behold, and He was ever pleasing to speak to, even ready under the sharpest pains to administer to the afflicted. Thus should we endeavor to comport ourselves under any trial we should have to endure. (78)

4. The virtue that seems to underlie all Catherine's oral instructions is humility, to which poverty of spirit was, in her thinking, intimately related. Humility is not talked about much today for fear people will think we are talking about external pseudo-humility, the kind one might put on so people will think one is "humble" or "holy." But when Catherine speaks about humility she is not talking about this or that external behavior, but about interior truthfulness about ourselves and detachment from ourselves. For her, such humility resembles in some way the anonymity of God's action. In one of her most moving sayings she counsels, "See how quietly the great God does all His mighty

works: darkness is spread over us at night and light returns in the morning, and there is no noise of closing shutters or drawing curtains."[12]

Catherine is therefore convinced that "the first and most essential virtue to acquire is humility.... It must emanate from the heart and arise from a deep conviction of our own nothingness and dependence on God, well knowing that if He withdraws His supporting hand we will immediately fall" (77). Elsewhere she says that humility "consists in having a thorough knowledge of ourselves, as we are in the sight of God, and of our inability to do the smallest thing without His assistance or that of others" (91). Therefore she asks:

> See then, are you truly humble, not in words or appearance only, but in deed. It is not enough to have a clear knowledge of one's insufficiency; we must also ... be willing that everyone should ... treat us as we deserve.... [I]f you feel hurt or annoyed when reminded of your faults ... or when you think the attention or respect due to [you] is not given you, you are far from possessing this necessary ... virtue. (138–39)

For Catherine poverty of spirit was intimately related to humility:

> To be poor in spirit does not consist in wearing poor clothes, and yet at the same time be covetous—covetous of praise, of preferment, of distinction.... We have also sworn ... to renounce pride, that is, a desire or wish to be considered something more than the rest ... to possess more influence, more knowledge, more talent, more piety, more ... of anything than another.... If this feeling of self-sufficiency or pride reigns in us, it will manifest itself in our conduct and manners. (111, 118)

Perhaps Catherine's most stark and comprehensive guidance on humility is expressed in the following words:

> Let us not ... suppose, however virtuous, talented, or useful we may be in the community, that our loss would be felt even for a moment. After

we are gone, everything will go on, no duty will be omitted, just as if we had never existed.... We should endeavor to feel quite indifferent to all these things, and remember, whether we are noticed now or not, the time will come in a few years when we and our actions will be forgotten and unknown. (72, 143)

So what are we to make of these instructions of Catherine McAuley, the woman Sisters of Mercy revere as their founder and inspiration? Is there a present-day relevance in what she teaches us in these instructions?

If what Catherine has said resembles the Gospel, if her words echo Jesus' own words, if they shed some light on his spirit and mode of life, then we probably ought to take them seriously as steps toward living a truly Christian and profoundly merciful life.

The founder of any Christian religious congregation or movement has an obligation to teach. It is her duty to share with her followers and others, however reticently, her understanding of the calling at the heart of the ecclesial community. To fulfill this duty, she may be helped by the enabling gifts of God's Spirit. Then what she says may be said to shine with some of the Light of Christ, some of the wisdom and values God wishes to see incarnated in God's people.

Catherine McAuley is, in the view of many, a canonizable saint. She has now, we trust, reached the homeland she desired. Her pilgrimage is over. But her mission on this earth is perhaps not ended, any more than is the mission of the Christ whom she so tried to resemble, and who is still at work among us: "And I, when I am lifted up from the earth, will draw all people to myself" (John 12:32).

Catherine never made, and never could have made, any comment about what might be her mission when she was "gone." Like

Jesus, she surrendered, empty-handed in death, to the incomprehensible Mystery whom we call "God." But she did say a few words at the end that may suggest her ongoing mission. On the day of her death (November 11, 1841), she "told little Sr. Camillus Byrn," her godchild, "to kiss her and go away, that she would see her again, as if to prevent her from weeping." And later that evening she told Sister Teresa Carton, "will you tell the Sisters to get a good cup of tea—I think the community room would be a good place—when I am gone, and to comfort one another—but God will comfort them."[13]

Perhaps Catherine McAuley's ongoing mission is to continue to be for all of us what she tried to be during her earthly pilgrimage: a shining human lamp, a comforting, guiding soul-friend, a servant of that definitive and incomparably Comforting Mercy that Walter Kasper calls "the source and the goal of God's ways" on our behalf[14]—until that day when we hope to enter fully into God's heavenly country. Perhaps Catherine's instructions presented in this volume can still be heard and can still help and comfort the whole pilgrim church who now call her Venerable.[15]

Endnotes

Part 1, Introduction

1. "Perfectae Caritatis: Decree on the Appropriate Renewal of the Religious Life," art. 2, in *The Documents of Vatican II*, ed. Walter M. Abbott (New York: America Press, 1966), 468.

2. Mary C. Sullivan, ed., *The Practical Sayings of Catherine McAuley* (Rochester, New York: Sisters of Mercy of the Americas, 2010), 3. This book is a reprint of Mary Clare Moore, comp., *A Little Book of Practical Sayings, Advices, and Prayers … of Mary Catharine* [*sic*] *McAuley* (London: Burns, Oates, 1868). Hereafter cited as *PS*.

3. Catherine McAuley, "The Spirit of the Institute" in *The Correspondence of Catherine McAuley, 1818–1841*, ed. Mary C. Sullivan (Washington, D.C.: The Catholic University of America Press, 2004), 462. *Correspondence* is hereafter cited as *CCMcA*.

4. In 2012, in the *Path of Mercy* (Washington, D.C.: The Catholic University of America Press, 2012), 387–89, I explained why I then regarded certain features of the manuscript's "Introduction" as problematic: its alleged authorship, as given by Degnan, and its claims about how the instructions were presented and recorded. In the text that follows I extend and only slightly modify my earlier views.

5. In the foreword to her 1952 publication, Degnan claims that the manuscript was compiled in Tullamore by Mary Teresa Purcell (who entered Baggot Street in 1834, moved to Tullamore in 1836, and died there in 1853). In the *Path of Mercy*, I have argued against attributing the "Introduction" of the compilation and the compilation itself to Teresa Purcell, on the grounds of Teresa's presumably greater familiarity with and understanding of the origin of the various instructions and their transcriptions as compared with that of whoever wrote the introduction, probably a sister who entered the Tullamore community and

may have heard few if any of the instructions directly from Catherine McAuley.

6. Interestingly, among the prepublication "Subscribers" to the 1806 Kilkenny edition (in English) of Rodriguez's three-volume work, which is apparently the edition Catherine McAuley used, are listed at least three of her close spiritual advisors: "Rev. Doctor [Thomas] Betagh, Dublin," "Rev. Mr. [Edward] Armstrong, Dublin," and "Rev. A[ndrew] Fitzgerald, Carlow."

7. In the *Path of Mercy* (153), I implied that Catherine McAuley herself may have composed the "Prayer for Patience" that she wrote on the flyleaf of her copy of Joseph Joy Dean's *Devotions to the Sacred Heart of Jesus.* I have since discovered that she transcribed this prayer from John Gother's *The Sinner's Complaints to God,* joining passages on two different pages of his book of prayers (215 and 355). Gother, *The Sinner's Complaints to God: Being Devout Entertainments of the Soul with God,* Birmingham, England: T. Holliwell, 1770.

8. Sometime before her death, Catherine McAuley gave Mary de Pazzi Delany a copy of Thomas à Kempis, *The Imitation of Christ.* On the front flyleaf of the book Catherine wrote, "To Sister Mary de Pazzi from her affectionate Mother in Christ." After Sister de Pazzi's death in 1872, the book was sent to Mary Clare Moore in Bermondsey, London, where it is now preserved in AIMGB. Clare says that Catherine's "Favourite Book" was "'The Following of Christ,' especially the Chapters 30th of Book 3rd, and 8th of Book 4th" (*PS,* 35).

9. Interestingly, a sentence, about living quietly with purity of intention, that Mary Vincent Harnett presents as one of Catherine McAuley's sayings is in Michel-Ange Marin's *The Perfect Religious* (Dublin: Depository of St. Mary's Asylum, 1845). Harnett gives Catherine's saying thus: "How silently and brilliantly the lamp in the Sanctuary burns, before the Most Holy Sacrament, when the oil is pure and good; it is only when it is otherwise that it twinkles and makes noise" (Mary C. Sullivan, *Catherine McAuley and the Tradition of Mercy* [Notre Dame, Ind.: University of Notre Dame Press, 1995], 174. Hereafter cited as *CMcATM*). Marin's wording in the 1845 edition is thus: "Be like a lamp which consumes itself without noise before the tabernacle; when a taper sparkles in burning, it is a proof that the wax of which it is composed is adulterated" (322–23).

10. Bermondsey Annals (1868) 1:[124], preserved in AIMGB. The Rule here mentioned is the Rule and Constitutions of the Religious Sisters of Mercy that Catherine McAuley composed in the early 1830s. It is preserved in CMA and is hereafter cited simply as Rule. Pope Gregory XVI confirmed the Rule in 1841, but the sequence of the chapters and some of the wording in the confirmed Rule differ from that in Catherine's composition.

11. *CMcATM,* 111.

12. Ibid., 116, 181.

13. Ibid., 107, 110, 117.

14. Ibid., 67.

15. *CCMcA,* 180, 205, 384.

16. "The Spirit of the Institute," in *CCMcA,* 461.

17. *CCMcA,* 323.

18. *CMcATM,* 181, 103.

19. Ibid., 201. Clare Augustine Moore may be referring to *The Sufferings of our Lord Jesus Christ* by Thomas of Jesus, or to the subtitle of Barthélémy Baudrand's *Soul on Calvary.*

20. Ibid., 230.

21. Rule II, 3.1, in *CMcATM,* 321.

22. Rule II, 6.1–8, in *CMcATM,* 323–25.

23. *CMcATM,* 168.

24. Catherine's essay is in *CCMcA,* 458–63. See also Mary C. Sullivan, "Catherine McAuley's Theological and Literary Debt to Alonso Rodriguez: The 'Spirit of the Institute' Parallels," in *Recusant History* (now, *British Catholic History*) 20 (May 1990): 81–105.

25. *CMcATM,* 100.

26. Teresa was often commanded by her directors or superiors to write about her experiences in prayer, and therefore did so. Catherine was apparently under no such obligation, and refrained from doing so.

27. *CCMcA,* 199.

28. Ibid., 156.

29. *CMcATM,* 105. However, in her handwritten copy of her profession of vows on December 12, 1831, Anna Maria Doyle gives her name in religion as "Sister Mary Ann Teresa."

30. Thereafter Catherine always called her niece "Mary Teresa."

31. *CMcATM,* 114, 178. When the Baggot Street income from various sources was adequate, even barely so, Catherine had a relaxed attitude toward dowries. She was always conscious of the often limited financial resources of the families from which the young women came.

32. "The Interior Castle," in Teresa of Avila, *Collected Works of St. Teresa of Avila,* trans. Kieran Kavanaugh and Otilio Rodriguez (Washington: Institute of Carmelite Studies Publications, 1980), 2:450, 449, 448.

33. "The Foundations," in Teresa of Avila, *Collected Works,* 3:117.

34. Report of Teresa's cousin Maria de San Gerónimo, in *The Complete*

Works of St. Teresa, trans. and ed. E. Allison Peers (London: Sheed and Ward, 1946, 1975), vol. 3: 351.

35. I am grateful to Elizabeth M. Davis, RSM, for her identification of the English version of the Bible that Catherine McAuley would have used.

36. *CMcATM*, 111.

37. Philip Sheldrake, *Spirituality and History: Questions of Interpretation and Method* (New York: Crossroad, 1992), 173. Sheldrake is discussing the interpretive approach of Hans-Georg Gadamer, *Truth and Method* (London: Sheed and Ward, 1979).

38. Mary Teresa Austin Carroll, *Leaves from the Annals of the Sisters of Mercy* (New York: Catholic Publication Society, 1881), 1:50.

39. "Dedication," Cork Manuscript 3, preserved in MCA.

40. "Spirit of the Institute," in *CCMcA*, 463.

41. Part 2, 42.

Pt. 2, ch 1

1. This paragraph and the following one show some influence from Louis Bourdaloue, SJ, *Spiritual Retreat for Religious Persons* (London: Keating and Brown, 1828). In Catherine McAuley's day, many comparable though not identical editions of his *Retreat* existed in English translation, including editions in 1810, 1828, 1830, 1833, and 1838. Some of these editions begin with God's invitation to solitude in the wilderness, as in Hosea 2:14; others, such as the 1828 edition (and Catherine's instructions), begin with Jesus' invitation to his disciples to come apart and rest in a deserted place, as in Mark 6:31. No further direct evidence of the influence of Bourdaloue's *Retreat* on Catherine's instructions has been discovered in chapter 1, but this *Retreat* heavily influences the content and wording of chapter 5.

2. This sentence is the first of twenty-seven "sayings" of Catherine McAuley that appear in chapter 1 of her compiled instructions. The phrasing and sequencing of the sayings here follow that in the Bermondsey manuscript numbered IOLM/BER/12/1/4, not that in Clare Moore's later collection of *The Practical Sayings … of Catharine* [*sic*] *McAuley* (1868) where the sayings are "classified under different heads—Humility—Charity, etc." according to the Bermondsey Annals (1868), 2:[136].

3. "As covetousness is the root of all evil, so poverty is the source and origin of all good … with respect to humility, St. Gregory says, that poverty is its guardian …. [H]oly men, speaking of poverty, call it sometimes the guardian

and mistress, at other times, the mother of virtues" (Rodriguez, *Practice,* 3:114).

4. "Our Saviour answers [St. Peter] ... 'you who have followed me ... shall sit also upon twelve seats.' .... It is the common opinion of holy men, that these words ought also to be extended to all those, who have imitated the apostles in voluntary poverty; and chiefly to those who have engaged themselves to it by vow, as all Religious do" (Rodriguez, *Practice,* 3:116).

5. "St. Gregory [says] ... 'St. Peter and St. Andrew left much; because they denied themselves even the desire and inclination of having any thing at all.' St. Austin [Augustine] ... says that 'the Apostles left all to follow Christ; because upon his call they had forsaken their nets and fishing-boat. And in effect, he [*sic*] really despises and leaves every thing, who quits and despises not only those things which he possessed, but all other things ... to which his desires might have carried him'" (Rodriguez, *Practice,* 3:121).

6. "This is St. Basil's doctrine in his explanation of these words of St. Paul, 'having food and raiment, let us be content.' Another Saint observes ... that St. Paul says, 'food and not delicacies, and raiment, to cover us, not to make us gay and fine.' ... Nay, we ought to desire the worst of every thing in the house ... the better to resemble Jesus Christ, 'who when he was rich became poor for our sakes'" (Rodriguez, *Practice,* 3:132, 133, 134).

7. "A holy man very justly compared chastity to a looking-glass, which is tarnished by the least breath. It is thus, the least thing tarnishes chastity, and makes it lose all its lustre" (Rodriguez, *Practice,* 3:163). Catherine says very little of what one might expect in instructions on the vow of chastity. Apparently she was not guided in her instructions, at least not extensively, by Rodriguez's commentary, which often displays a fear of women. His treatise on Chastity, in *Practice* 3:158–91, tends to focus largely on the human perils of celibate chastity, on the range of sins against purity, and on the strict asceticism required to overcome these grave difficulties. Catherine focuses more positively on resemblance to Jesus Christ (in simplicity, modesty of manner, silence, humility, watchfulness), on similarity to the angels (also in Rodriguez's treatise), and on the graces and favors Christ grants to those who profess this vow.

8. "To live in fear, to diffide in ourselves, and to fix all our confidence in God alone, conduce very much to maintain a pure spirit, and to preserve ourselves in the grace of God" (Rodriguez, *Practice,* 3:181).

9. In *Practice,* vol. 3, Rodriguez's treatise on Obedience begins with a chapter on the "Excellency of the virtue of obedience" (192–96).

10. "St. Thomas [Aquinas] ... asks whether obedience be the chief and principal vow made in religion; and having answered himself in the affirmative,

he proves his assertion by these three following reasons.... The first is, that by the vow of obedience, we offer more to God, than by the other vows. By the vow of poverty we sacrifice our riches, by that of chastity, our body, but by obedience we offer up our will and understanding; and entirely sacrifice the whole man to God; which undoubtedly is the noblest sacrifice of the three.... The second reason ... is because [obedience] really includes the other virtues.... For though a Religious bind himself by the ... vows of poverty and chastity, yet both these obligations are contained in the vow of obedience, by which he is obliged in general to observe all that shall be commanded him [in the Rule].... The third reason is this ... it is obedience, which most unites Religious with the end [purpose] of their institution ... it commands us to labour for our own, and our neighbour's spiritual advancement.... St. Thomas draws a conclusion from hence ... viz., that the very essence and soul of a religious life, consists chiefly in the vow of obedience ... it is obedience which makes Religious, and places them in a religious state. St. Bonaventure ... says, that the perfection of a religious man, consists in denying his own will, and following the will of another" (Rodriguez, *Practice,* 3:193–94).

11. "Obedience is the virtue which essentially constitutes religion, and properly makes a Religious.... [I]t is this that comprises not only poverty and chastity, but all other virtues also" (Rodriguez, *Practice,* 3:195). See also note 10 above.

12. "Whereas those who have devoted themselves to obedience, have sacrificed their will to God, who esteems no sacrifice like that of the liberty of our will; man having nothing more noble or precious to offer him" (Rodriguez, *Practice,* 3:223).

13. "We must consider, that if it be a part of prudence, not to trust our own judgment too far in any thing we do; much more ought it to be so, when our own interest is in question; it being a maxim in morality that no man is a proper judge in his own case" (Rodriguez, *Practice,* 3:228).

14. St. Basil "says thus, 'do not think that I presume of myself to make this comparison. No! I take it from our holy faith, and the authority of Christ himself, who says, he that hears you, hears me', that is, he that obeys you, obeys me. All the Holy Fathers give the same interpretation of these words, and say, that they are to be understood not only of the apostles, but of all superiors and spiritual directors" (Rodriguez, *Practice,* 3:237). This passage is in chapter 11 of Rodriguez's treatise on obedience. Clare Moore's manuscript biography of Catherine McAuley says that "the first public lecture [Catherine] read after being appointed Mother Superior [December 13, 1831] was the tenth Chapter of

Rodriguez on Obedience—being an explanation of St. Paul's words 'Obey your Prelates and be subject to them for they watch continually being to give an account for your souls'" (*CMcATM,* 108). Presumably Catherine read more to the community than simply chapter 10.

15. Rodriguez discusses "three degrees of perfection" with respect to obedience in *Practice,* 3:199–209.

16. "St. John Climacus calls 'obedience the tomb of our will, wherein it lies dead, and from which humility rises again'" (Rodriguez, *Practice,* 3:203–4).

17. "All those, says he [St. Ignatius], that live under obedience, must know, that they are to suffer themselves to be led, and guided, as Divine Providence shall direct, by the hand of their superior, just as a dead corpse, which permits itself to be moved and carried where you please" (Rodriguez, *Practice,* 3:212).

18. The three preceding sentences show the influence of Rodriguez: "St. Ignatius adds ... that we must not consider whether it be the superior, or one in authority under him, that commands, since we obey God, not them. He would also have us obey all under-officers, with as much respect, readiness, and resignation, as the superior himself" (*Practice,* 3:241).

19. Here and in the following paragraph Catherine is speaking about charity toward the women sheltered and trained at the House of Mercy in the convent on Baggot Street, Dublin.

20. In his treatise "Of Union and Fraternal Charity," Rodriguez discusses St. Ignatius's view that the Society of Jesus "is like a battalion of soldiers," and the church, according to St. Bernard, is "Terrible as an army ranged in battle." "If we preserve the spirit of union, if we assist one another, if we march well united ... we shall infallibly overcome, and be under no apprehension of defeat in any encounter.... Even so will Religious be strong, when they are all united with one another, by the bond of fraternal charity.... By this means we shall advance in perfection.... The devil himself will tremble" (*Practice,* 1:142–43).

21. The Bermondsey manuscript numbered IOLM/BER/12/1/4, an *archetype* for this entire chapter of the compiled manuscript, has "unwearied" here. Perhaps "unvaried" is a copyist's error.

22. The following date is in the compiled manuscript, as here.

Pt. 2, ch. 2

1. "'He that contemneth small things ... shall fall little by little' [Eccles. 19:1]. The doctrine contained in these words is of great importance to all persons especially to those who aspire to perfection; for we are exact in the performance

of great things, as they carry with themselves their own recommendation, but it is very usual with us to be careless in small things, as we fancy they are of no consequence. In this, however, we deceive ourselves, because it is very dangerous to neglect and fail in these things; and therefore the Holy Ghost in this passage of Scripture declares to us, 'That he who contemns small things, shall fall by little and little.' To convince us then of this truth, and to oblige us to be watchful, it ought to be sufficient that God himself says so" (Rodriguez, *Practice,* 1:37–38). Note that Catherine McAuley inserts "(not *may*)" after "shall" in the quotation of Sirach (Ecclesiasticus) 19:1, on which Rodriguez comments.

2. In her commentary on Luke 16.10, which follows, Catherine seems to echo Rodriguez's comments: "I cannot comprehend how any person, who … persists even in one fault, how trivial soever it may appear, can lift up his eyes … to beg of God new and extraordinary graces …. he who makes good use of the grace he has received deserves to obtain new ones; but on the contrary, he who does not employ the first well, becomes undeserving of any more" (*Practice,* 1:45–46).

3. The quotations from Rodriguez's *Practice* that are cited in notes 1 and 2 are transformed in Catherine McAuley's manuscript transcription of these chapters of Rodriguez into language that more closely matches the language she uses here in her "instructions." This suggests that Catherine is here following her own altered transcription of Rodriguez (numbered CMA/1/5/1 and preserved in MCA), rather than his printed text.

4. The preceding paragraph may reflect the influence of Michel-Ange Marin's passage in *The Perfect Religious,* 144–45: "Do not think that your talents, however great they may be, render you so useful to your community as that it cannot subsist without you. Your monastery subsisted before you were received into it, and will not perish when you shall be no more. There were Religious in it much superior to you; they have died, and nevertheless the monastery has not decayed with them. When you die, do you think it will perish with you? Religion requires, in general, the members of which it is composed, though no person in particular, but each individual cannot secure her happiness without it. How great would be your illusion, if, under pretext of your good qualities, you thought yourself necessary as the only support of your community? … A religious, who is truly humble …. would regard it as a ridiculous idea to consider herself necessary in her community, much less speak in a manner to make others think her so."

5. "If you be without religious virtues, and have only the exterior marks of religion, you resemble a tree loaded with leaves and blossoms, but which bears

no fruit; and it is those fruits of virtue and life that God wishes to find in you" (Marin, *Perfect Religious,* 66).

6. The preceding paragraph and the inclusion of the following verse from Psalm 45 may reflect the influence and wording of Bourdaloue, *Spiritual Retreat for Religious Persons,* 192, 193–94: "Our perfection in the sight of God does not consist in doing many things.... It does not consist in doing great things. Many eminent saints have done nothing great in the eyes of men .... Perfection does not require the performance of singular or extraordinary things—such occasions seldom occur.... The perfection of our ordinary actions chiefly springs from the interior spirit, or principal motive with which they are performed.... Hence the Royal Prophet says: 'All the glory of the king's daughter is within.'" See the *Jerome Biblical Commentary,* ed. Raymond E. Brown, Joseph A. Fitzmyer, and Roland E. Murphy (Englewood Cliffs, N.J.: Prentice-Hall, 1968), 583–84, for a contemporary exegesis of Psalm 45.

7. "All therefore consists in beginning well, as St. Bonaventure teaches .... St. John Climacus also says, 'that loose and weak beginnings are very dangerous, this being an evident sign of a future fall'" (Rodriguez, *Practice,* 1:95).

8. This paragraph and the following one may have been influenced by Rodriguez's chapter, "Of the imitation of Jesus Christ, which is the chief advantage ... from the meditation of his life and passion" (*Practice,* 2:363–65). Rodriguez writes: "The imitation of the virtues of Jesus Christ is ... what we ought to propose to ourselves, in the meditations of his passion, and the fruit we are to endeavour to reap from thence.... His whole life was a perfect model of all virtues, which he seemed to teach us both by his words and actions, yet ... to collect them all together in his passion ... so that what we ought to endeavour to draw from the meditation on his sufferings, is an ardent desire of imitating his virtues. For this end, we must apply ourselves to examine at leisure each virtue separately.... In short, we must run over, in the same manner, all the virtues, as obedience, charity, meekness, chastity, poverty, abstinence, and the rest ... and we must then exercise ourselves in framing in our hearts, a true desire of imitating and practicing them.... [I]n meditating on the life and passion of Jesus Christ, the imitation of him ought to be our chief entertainment, and the chief fruit we are to endeavour to reap from it. But to do this, each one is very much to insist upon the imitation of the virtue he finds himself to stand most in need of.... [A]fter this we may pass to another virtue, and from thence to a third; and without doubt it is far better and more profitable to observe this method, than to embrace many things together in prayer, and to pass but slightly over them all."

9. This sentence as well as much of the advice contained in the following instructions on "20th July" and "21st July" (below), up to the section that begins with "Six defects . . . ," is strongly dependent on the wording, content, and emphases contained in Catherine McAuley's own archetypal hand-printed manuscript, which is contained on pages 45–102 of a leather-bound copybook numbered CMA/1/5/2 and preserved in MCA. This reliance is not continual, but her hand-printed thoughts appear very frequently in these pages of the compiled manuscript and in sequence. However, the specific source, if there was one, of her thoughts as expressed in that archetypal manuscript has not so far been discovered. Her thoughts here may rely, in general, on Rodriguez's *Practice,* but this has not been determined.

10. The "six defects" to be avoided in receiving visits in the parlor, as presented in the following paragraphs, may reflect some influence from Marin's treatment of this topic (*Perfect Religious,* 16–18). However, Catherine's wording, as given here, seems less fearful of such visits than Marin's, and more reasonable and charitable toward the visitors. This is the only place in the compiled manuscript of her oral instructions where she deals with this matter. Both Birmingham MS GB/1858/10/100/4/1 (Hardman's manuscript) and Naas Manuscript C9/4/4 contain wording that is very similar to this passage.

11. This entire paragraph relies on wording in Rodriguez, *Practice,* 2:333–38: "'If then,' says St. Bernard, 'you would banish sadness far from you, and live always content, live as you ought to do. Think what your obligations are, and apply yourself to the performance of them.' . . . [T]here cannot be a more sensible joy, than they feel who have the testimony of a good conscience. 'There is not a greater pleasure,' says the Scripture, '[it] is like a continual feast.' . . . St. Chrysostom also assures us that a good conscience dissipates all darkness of heart, and drives it away, as the sun does the clouds; and that sadness which falls upon a good conscience, is as easily extinguished, as a spark of fire that falls into a lake. . . . [O]ne reason . . . why St. Francis desired always to see cheerfulness in the countenances of his Religious, was because he looked upon this joy 'as one of the fruits of the Holy Ghost.' . . . Cassian as well as [St. Basil] established two sorts of sadness, the one purely human, and according to the spirit of the world; the other spiritual, and according to the spirit of God. . . . Jesus Christ himself was touched at the death of Lazarus; and therefore the Jews cried out when they saw him weep, 'behold how he loved him.' . . . [S]piritual sadness . . . may proceed from a sight of our sins . . . from a consideration of the many sins daily committed in the world . . . [from] perceiving we make so little progress in virtue. . . . [T]he joy required in the servants of God, is not a vain and frivo-

lous one; it is not a joy that makes us break out into loud laughter.... For this would not be a joy becoming God's servants.... The joy we require is a prudent one, that comes from within; and is visible in our countenance ... according to the expression of Scripture, 'a sad mind dries up the bones' (Prov. 17.22) ... [and] according to this other passage of scripture: 'a joyful heart gives a cheerful countenance' (Prov. 15.13)." Birmingham MS GB 1858/10/100/4/1, handwritten by Catherine McAuley, contains the quotations in this paragraph, and obviously relies on the wording and content of Rodriquez, *Practice,* 2:333–38.

12. There is no "of Sales" in Rodriguez's text or in Catherine's own transcription of this passage. Apparently the scribe of an *archetype* or of the compiled manuscript assumed that Rodriguez was citing the bishop of Geneva (1567–1622), whose spiritual works may not have been available to Rodriguez (1526–1616), when he was actually citing the saint of Assisi whose sayings and legends were available.

13. Despite extensive searching I have not been able to find in scripture or elsewhere the source of the scriptural claim Catherine makes in this last sentence and in other places in her oral instructions.

Part 2, ch. 3

1. Chapter 2 has a "13th July" entry; chapter 3 does not. See Editor's Note.

2. "If in the beginning of your conversion, when novelty should increase your fervour and zeal, you notwithstanding languish and become tepid, what will become of you when your ears shall be accustomed and your heart hardened to all things that may touch you or do you any good?" (Rodriguez, *Practice,* 1:94).

3. Chapter 2 has a "16th July" entry; chapter 3 does not. See Editor's Note.

4. The two preceding paragraphs on the importance of the novitiate period appear to depend somewhat on the content and emphases in Rodriguez's chapter 9 on the importance of the noviceship (*Practice,* 1:93–97).

5. "Another means ... which will serve to encourage us still more, is, that we should always imagine we have a great way to go, and that as yet we have advanced but very little. Our blessed Saviour also insinuates the adoption of this means by these words, 'Be ye perfect as your heavenly Father is perfect.' For what, think you, does our Saviour mean by saying so? Can it be, that we should ever be able to come near the perfection of our heavenly Father? ... No, certainly.... And yet our Saviour says to us, 'Be perfect as our heavenly Father is perfect,' to let us understand that in the career of virtue there are no bounds,

and therefore we should never be satisfied with what we have already done, but should labour continually to acquire what we still want" (Rodriguez, *Practice,* 1:61–62).

6. The second scriptural passage in this sentence is in St. Paul's sermon in Antioch (Acts 14.22), where it is not attributed to Jesus.

7. "St. Chrysostom adds, that what we ought with all zeal and care to procure, is to be esteemed by God; and since the esteem or contempt of men can neither give nor take anything from us, we have no reason to trouble ourselves about what opinion they entertain of us.... Let us add to this a consideration of St. Bonaventure: Be not angry, says he, with those that speak ill of you: for either what they say is true or false: if it is true, you must not wonder they dare say what you durst do; if it is false, their detraction can do you no harm" (Rodriguez, *Practice,* 1:109).

8. "But, because we cannot always hide our good actions, this being impossible for those who are obliged to contribute by their example to the edification of their neighbour; the first means of defence against vainglory, is to rectify in the beginning our intention, and to elevate our heart to God, and offer him all our thoughts, words, and actions; to the end, that when vainglory comes to claim a part in them, we may say to it, according to the advice of Father [John of] Avila, 'You come too late, all is already given to God.' It will also be very good to make use of the answer St. Bernard made to a thought of vainglory ... 'I neither began,' says he, 'for your sake, nor will I leave off for it'" (Rodriguez, *Practice,* 1:111).

9. "All the Saints admonish us to be on our guard against vainglory; because say they, it is a cunning thief, which often steals from us our best actions; and which insinuates itself so very secretly.... St. Gregory says, that vainglory is like a robber, who first craftily insinuates himself into the company of a traveller, pretending to go the same way he does and afterwards robs and kills him when he is least upon his guard, and when he thinks himself in greatest security" (Rodriguez, *Practice,* 1:99).

188 Part 2, ch. 4

1. "Ponder the tender feelings with which Jesus Christ expresses his desire of consummating the Paschal ceremony.... See him preparing himself and his disciples for this great event, by an act of profound humility—behold him girding himself, pouring water into a basin, bending, and washing the feet of his imperfect disciples ... and let his divine example on this occasion, be your model,

whenever charity or obedience shall employ you in any humiliating office.... Admire, especially, his humility in washing the feet of the traitor.... Ponder the benign expression with which Jesus concluded this great lesson of humility" (Bourdaloue, *Spiritual Retreat for Religious Persons,* 1828 edition, 98–99). Many passages in Rodriguez, *Practice,* describe Jesus washing his disciples' feet, but Bourdaloue's passage seems closest to Catherine's wording.

2. Catherine McAuley's instructions "On the Passion of Jesus Christ" (in this first long section of chapter 4) may rely, in general, on Barthélémy Baudraud's *Elevation of the Soul to God* (in particular, its chapter on the Passion) and his *Soul on Calvary,* a book entirely devoted to the sufferings of Christ during his Passion. No other possible source for this section of chapter 4 has so far been discovered.

3. Here St. John Climacus is actually quoting St. Paul (2 Cor. 6.10).

4. In Richard Challoner, *Journal of Meditations for Every Day in the Year,* a book from which Catherine read daily to the Baggot Street community, part of the meditation for "Ash-Wednesday. Our Lord's Sermon after the Last Supper" reads: "'If you love me' saith he, 'keep my commandments.' And again, 'If any one love me, he will keep my word.' 'The proof therefore of love,' saith St. Gregory, 'is the performance of deeds'" (132).

5. The following passage is in Rodriguez, *Practice* (1:352–53): "'You have created us, O Lord, for yourself, and our heart will never be at rest till it reposes in you' [Augustine, *Confessions,* Book 1, ch. 1]. The comparison usually made, of the needle of a compass, is very applicable, and explains exceedingly well the words of St. Austin. The property of this needle when touched on the load-stone, is, to turn always to the north: and the impression and virtue it receives by this touch is so forcible, that move it which way you please, it never ceases to be in agitation, till it has recovered its first direction. It is the same with us, in respect of God. He has inspired into us a natural inclination, which carries us continually to him, as to our north pole and our last end. So that as long as our heart turns not to God, so long like this needle shall we be in continual motion and disquiet.... But as soon as it [the needle] has found the fixed and immovable north pole it stands still and immovable. Just so, as long as your eyes and heart are cast upon the things of this world, which are subject to daily alterations and changes, you will never have repose and satisfaction; but turn them towards God, who is unalterable and still the same, and you will obtain a perfect joy and tranquility."

See also the following passage in Luis de Granada, *The Sinner's Guide* (Philadelphia: Henry McGrath, [1844]), 265–66: "[It is impossible for a person] to find any rest but in God, who has been created for none but God. That you may understand this the better, look on the needle of the compass, and there you will see a lively figure of this necessary doctrine. The nature of this needle is to point always to the north, when it has been once touched to the loadstone: God, who created this stone, gave it such a natural inclination to turn always that way.... It is not to be doubted, but that God has created man with the same natural inclination and tendency toward him, as toward his pole, his centre and his last end; and therefore it is, that, like the needle, he is continually disturbed and unquiet, as long as he is turned from God, though he should enjoy all the riches in the world; but as soon as, like the needle, he returns to him, he ceases from his violent motion, and enjoys perfect and entire rest, because it is in God he is to find his peace. Whence we may infer, that he alone is happy who possesses God; and that the nearer a man is to God, the nearer he is to this happiness."

6. "Martha and Mary are sisters—one neither hurts nor hinders the other; that is, action and contemplation prejudice not each other. But on the contrary, prayer well made helps us to perform each action well; and each action well done helps us very much to pray well.... Martha is troubled because her sister Mary does not help her.... Do you also endeavour to gain assistance from Mary, that is from prayer and meditation, and you will find that all your disquiet will soon vanish.... [T]hose who make profession of a spiritual life, ought not to act but under the shadow of contemplation; and must unite meditation and action in such manner, that the one be never separated from the other. Cassian says, that the ancient anchorets ... were most attentive to their work; and as long as their hands were employed in the duties of Martha, their hearts were entirely engaged in the exercises of Mary..... It is therefore by no means true that exterior occupations impede devotion, and interior recollection; on the contrary, they contribute thereto. For they giving employment but to the body, the mind is quite at liberty to think constantly on God" (Rodriguez, *Practice,* 1:115–16).

Part 2, chap. 5

1. The Rule referred to here is the "Rule and Constitutions of the Religious Sisters of Mercy" composed by Catherine McAuley in the 1830s and confirmed by Gregory XVI on June 6, 1841. In the years before the 1841 confirmation, manuscript copies of this proposed rule, as approved by Dublin Archbishop Daniel Murray, were available in all the early Mercy convents. Cf. commentary in *CMcATM,* 259–91.

2. Rule 1.1, in *CMcATM*, 295.

3. Final, unnumbered paragraph of the Rule, in *CMcATM*, 328.

4. Rule 2.1, in *CMcATM*, 296.

5. Rule 2.2, in *CMcATM*, 296, reads: "Before the Sisters enter School they shall raise their hearts to God and to the Queen of Heaven, recommending themselves and the Children to their care and protection. They shall endeavour to inspire them with a sincere Devotion to the Passion of Jesus Christ, to His real presence in the Most Holy Sacrament, to the Immaculate Mother of God, and their Guardian Angels."

6. Rule 2.3 and 2.4, in *CMcATM*, 296.

7. Rule 2.5, in *CMcATM*, 297.

8. "Of the Admission of Distressed Women," Rule 4, in *CMcATM*, 299–300.

9. "Of the Visitation of the Sick," Rule 3, in *CMcATM*, 297–99.

10. See note 8 above. Although the House of Mercy at Baggot Street did not accept women who had engaged in a life of prostitution, some of the homeless domestic servants it did admit may have been sexually harassed or molested by male members in the households of their previous employers.

11. I cannot confidently identify the sister who gives her initials after this parenthetical comment on Catherine's views. If the initials are "Sr. M. C. L.," she may be Mary Catherine Locke, who entered the Tullamore community in 1836 and remained there until 1848, when she went to Derry. If they are "Sr. M. C. D.," she may be Clare Delamere who entered the Tullamore community in 1836 and was its annalist until she went to Kells in 1844. See Sullivan, *Path of Mercy*, 389n28.

12. Beginning with this paragraph at least twenty-seven (27) "practical sayings" of Catherine McAuley are embedded in the text of chapter 5. Since the Bermondsey manuscript IOLM/BER/12/1/4 (presumably composed by Mary Clare Moore, who also later published *A Little Book of Practical Sayings, Advices and Prayers of … Catharine* [*sic*] *McAuley* in 1868) is one of the *archetypes* of chapter 5 (see Editor's Note), the large number of Catherine's "sayings" that appear here is not surprising. See this volume's introduction for an explanation of the probable sequence and timing of Clare Moore's compositions.

13. Intermittent dependence on the wording and content of Mary Gonzaga O'Brien's notebook begins here. See the Editor's Note to chapter 5 for an account of Mary Gonzaga's relation to Frances Warde, and the character and location of her notebook.

14. "St. Bernard observes, that there are two sorts of humility; one in the understanding, whereby man considering his misery and lowliness is so convinced thereof, that he despises himself, and believes that he deserves to be

altogether contemned; the other in the will, which makes him desire to be despised and disesteemed by all the world" (Rodriguez, *Practice,* 2:162).

15. "It is not enough therefore to have a contempt of yourself, and to speak ill of yourself even from your heart, you must endeavour to attain the point of being willing that others should think and say of you, what you think and say of yourself, and be content that they effectually despise you" (Rodriguez, *Practice,* 2:158–59).

16. "By the predominant passion is meant, that vice which has the greatest sway over our hearts.... The necessity of discovering this vice is obvious; without it, the foundation of a truly virtuous life cannot well be laid.... Hence proceed our daily imperfections, faults, and sins.... Is it pride, sloth, vanity, envy, jealousy, inordinate love of creatures, or of yourself, etc. etc." (Bourdaloue, *Spiritual Retreat for Religious Persons,* 177–78).

17. In keeping with Ignatian tradition, Rodriguez (*Practice,* 1:303–36) devotes eleven chapters to his treatise "Of the Examen of Conscience." While Catherine shares his regard for this important religious practice, her treatment of it is much shorter; only occasionally does she use words or concepts found in his text.

18. "Scripture says of David, when he was encamped in sight of the Philistines, and his whole army was in great want of water: 'Oh that any one would get me some of the water of the fountain of Bethlem' which was beyond the enemies' camp. Whereupon three brave soldiers ... departed presently ... and brought to David the water of this fountain. But the Scripture adds, 'that he would not drink of it; but made a sacrifice of effusion to our Lord, by pouring it forth, and offering it unto him.' Is it therefore so great a sacrifice to offer a pot of water to our Lord? Yes, says St. Ambrose, it was a great sacrifice.... But would you know ... in what the greatness of this action consists? 'He overcame nature by not drinking in an extreme thirst....' It was not only the pot of water he offered, but it was his own will; and therefore in mortifying ourselves, though in ever so small things, it is the will always that is sacrificed unto God" (Rodriguez, *Practice,* 2:52–3).

19. In a section of *Spiritual Retreat* titled "Of the Manner of Performing our Daily Actions," Bourdaloue writes: "Among your daily actions, the most important are those which regard God.... Such are your morning exercises, your meditation, examination of conscience, vocal prayers, spiritual reading, hearing mass, and approaching the holy communion, and reciting the divine office.... The second class of ordinary duties regards your neighbour, and principally your sisters. Your intercourse with them will always prove a fruitful source of

occasions to deny yourself. What is the perfection to which you aspire on this point? Is it not ... to edify all by modesty, affability, and evenness of temper.... The third class of your daily duties regards yourself; these are trifling in themselves, but when animated by the spirit of obedience and self-denial, they are truly seeds of eternal life. Review your ordinary actions, your rising, dressing, meals, conversation, your whole exterior ... your appearance, conduct, or manners" (186–88). Catherine uses Bourdaloue's wording in her paragraph above, and then in the long commentary that follows she adds her own descriptive words to his list of the "daily duties [as] regards yourself."

20. So far it has proved impossible to find an exact source for Catherine's claim that "our Redeemer ... was always pleasing to behold and never sad or troublesome." She also makes this claim in chapter 1 of her instructions: "It is said of our Divine Lord that He was always pleasing to behold"; three times in chapter 2: "He was never sad or troublesome, but of a meek and sweet exterior which beautified His countenance and excited the admiration of all who beheld Him"; "His sufferings never caused Him to be sad or gloomy. His countenance was at all times delightful to behold"; and "the Scripture says His countenance was at *all times* pleasing to behold"; and in chapter 3: "His meekness and calm beautified His divine countenance and excited the admiration of all who beheld it." In speaking of conformity to the will of God, Rodriguez cites St. Catherine of Siena, who apparently made a somewhat similar claim about Jesus: "St. Catherine of Siena speaks admirably well upon this point in comparing the just to our Saviour Jesus Christ. For as Jesus Christ never lost the beatitude of his soul, amidst all the torments, sorrows, and anguishes he underwent; so the just, whatever afflictions, whatever adversities happen, never lose that beatitude which consists in a conformity to the divine will. Because the accomplishment of that will in them is always a new subject of joy" (*Practice,* 1:347–48).

21. In this sentence and the next three paragraphs Catherine is relying on Bourdaloue's wording: "Resolve to perform every exercise and every duty with exactness, fervour, and perseverance; for without these qualities, no action can be perfect. Exactness implies punctuality to every duty whatsoever, allotting to each its due time, and performing it in the manner and place prescribed. Fervor may be felt in sensible consolations; but as true fervor consists principally in a will determined to serve God at any rate, it may be experienced in the midst of trials, disgusts, and aridities. When these trials are endured with patience and humility, or when they are surmounted by purity of intention, and generous efforts in the divine service, the soul may be then said to be truly fervent. Perseverance is fervor, not merely in some duties, but in every duty.... Regularity is a

constant exercise of self-denial, and will keep your soul in continual subjection to God.... If your present dispositions be such as they ought to be, you will not close this consideration without exciting an unbounded confidence in God, and an ardent desire of perfection" (*Spiritual Retreat,* 174–75, 176–77).

22. "Many external graces are effectual means of sanctity and perfection in the religious life; such are the daily exercise of mental and vocal prayer, the frequent use of the sacraments, copious instructions, exhortations, spiritual lectures, retreats, charitable admonitions, and good example.... Wo [*sic*] to you, if they produce no fruit of solid virtue in the soil of your heart!" (Bourdaloue, *Spiritual Retreat,* 198).

23. "There are persons who outwardly seem to have the spirit of meekness and humility, so long as nothing thwarts them, and all things happen as they wish; but upon the least cross accident that occurs, this peace vanishes, and they presently take fire, and discover what they are. Such men as those, says Albertus [Magnus], have not the virtue of peace and humility in their own, but in other men's minds and humours; so that if your virtue be such as this, it belongs to others and not to you, since it lies in their power to give, or take it from you, whensoever they please. But your virtue, if it be true, must be your own, and not of another's growth, and the fund ought always to be at your own disposal, without any dependence upon another" (Rodriguez, *Practice,* 1:65–66).

24. "Good purposes are the result of serious reflections, grounded on faith and made in the presence of God. The object of good purposes, is to correct whatever appears defective in our moral or religious conduct, and to establish ourselves in the regular practice of solid virtues" (Bourdaloue, *Spiritual Retreat,* 194–95).

25. "Self-love is the cause of all evils and sins, and by consequence of hell itself. 'If there were no self-love,' says St. Bernard, 'there would be no hell'" (Rodriguez, *Practice,* 2:54).

26. "Time is most precious, because it is the price of eternity.... Time is never well spent, unless it is employed for the greater glory of God, and your own sanctification; all that is allotted to other purposes is irrevocably lost" (Bourdaloue, *Spiritual Retreat,* 180).

Part 3

1. Where page numbers are given in the text of this part 3 with no other reference, they refer to pages in part 2 of the present volume.

2. Pope Francis, *The Joy of the Gospel (Evangelii gaudium)* (Frederick, Md.: Word Among Us Press, 2013), art. 111.

3. Nicholas Lash, *Theology for Pilgrims* (Notre Dame, Ind.: University of Notre Dame Press, 2008), 270.

4. Bernard of Clairvaux, *On the Song of Songs,* vol. 3, trans. Kilian Walsh, OCSO, and Irene M. Edmonds (Kalamazoo, Mich.: Cistercian Publications, 1979), Sermon 59.3, 123.

5. Karl Rahner, *Watch and Pray with Me,* trans. William V. Dych (New York: Herder and Herder, 1966), 58.

6. Rule 3.6, in *CMcATM,* 298.

7. Rule 1.1, in *CMcATM,* 295.

8. "The Spirit of the Institute," in *CCMcA,* 462.

9. *PS,* 3.

10. *PS,* 16.

11. *CMcATM,* 117.

12. *PS,* 2.

13. *CMcATM,* 256, 243.

14. Walter Kasper, *Mercy: The Essence of the Gospel and the Key to Christian Life,* trans. William Madges (New York and Mahwah, N.J.: Paulist Press, 2014), 97.

15. According to the decree titled "Congregatio de Causis Sanctorum Decretum Dublinen. Canonizationis Servae Dei Catharinae McAuley Fundatricis Sororum a Misericordia (1778–1841)," on April 9, 1990, Pope John Paul II, in the presence of members of the Congregation for the Causes of Saints, read the following proclamation: "It is an established fact that the Servant of God Catherine McAuley, foundress of the Sisters of Mercy, practiced to a heroic degree the theological virtues of Faith, Hope, and Charity toward God and neighbor, and along with them the cardinal virtues of Prudence, Justice, Temperance, and Fortitude." The Holy Father then ordered that this decree be published and entered into the records of the Congregation for the Causes of Saints. Given at Rome, 9 April, A. D. 1990. [Signed] Angelo Cardinal Felici, Prefect, [Signed] + Edward Nowak, Titular Archbishop of Luni, Secretary." With the publication of this decree on her heroic virtues, Catherine McAuley may be referred to as "Venerable." In later stages of the process of canonization, the titles "Blessed" (beatification) and "Saint" (canonization) are conferred.

Bibliography

Baudrand, [Barthélémy]. *The Soul on Calvary, Meditating on the Sufferings of Jesus Christ.* Dublin: Catholic Book Society, 1840.

———. *Elevation of the Soul to God.* Translated by R. P[lowden]. 6th ed., rev. and corrected by F. J. L'Estrange. Dublin: Richard Coyne, 1824; 10th ed., Dublin: James Duffy, 1842.

Bellamy, Kathrine E. *Weavers of the Tapestry.* St. John's, Newfoundland: Flanker Press, 2006.

———. *The Steadfast Woman: The Story of Mary Francis Creedon.* [St. John's, Newfoundland]: Sisters of Mercy, n.d.

Bernard of Clairvaux. *On the Song of Songs.* Vol. 3. Translated by Kilian Walsh, OCSO, and Irene M. Edmonds. Kalamazoo, Michigan: Cistercian Publications, 1979.

Beyond Catherine: Stories of Mercy Foundresses. Dublin: Mercy International Association, 2003.

Blyth, Francis. *A Devout Paraphrase on the Seven Penitential Psalms: or, A Practical Guide to Repentance.* 7th ed. Dublin: Catholic Book Society, 1835.

Bourdaloue, Louis. *Spiritual Retreat for Religious Persons.* London: Keating and Brown, 1828.

Brennan, Bonaventure. *"It commenced with two . . .": The Story of Mary Ann Doyle.* N.p.: Sisters of Mercy of the Northern Province, Ireland, 2001.

Butler, Alban. *The Lives of the Fathers, Martyrs, and other Principal Saints.* 12 vols. New York: D. & J. Sadlier, 1846.

Carroll, Mary Teresa Austin. *Leaves from the Annals of the Sisters of Mercy.* Vol. 1. New York: Catholic Publication Society, 1881.

Bibliography

[Challoner, Richard, ed.]. *A Journal of Meditations for Every Day in the Year: Gathered Out of Divers Authors.* Dublin: Richard Coyne, 1823.

Davis, Elizabeth M. "Wisdom and Mercy Meet: Catherine McAuley's Interpretation of Scripture." In *Recovering Nineteenth-Century Women Interpreters of the Bible,* edited by Christiana de Groot and Marion Ann Taylor, 63–80. Atlanta: Society of Biblical Literature, 2007.

Dean, Joseph Joy, ed. *Devotions to the Sacred Heart of Jesus: Exercises for the Holy Sacrifice of the Mass, Confession and Communion.* Translated from the French. Dublin: Chambers and Hallagan, 1820.

[Degnan, Mary Bertrand, ed.]. *Retreat Instructions of Mother Mary Catherine McAuley by Sister Mary Teresa Purcell.* Westminster, Md.: Newman Press, 1952.

Form of Ceremony for the Reception and Profession of the Sisters of Our Lady of Mercy. Dublin: J. Byrn, 1834; London: C. Richards, 1840.

Francis. *The Joy of the Gospel (Evangelii gaudium).* Frederick, Md.: Word Among Us Press, 2013.

Gahan, William A. *The Christian's Guide to Heaven, or, A Complete Manual of Catholic Piety.* Dublin: T. M'Donnel, 1804; N.p.: Agra Press, 1834; Dublin: James Duffy, 1844. Cited as *Catholic Piety.*

Gother, John. *The Sinner's Complaints to God: Being Devout Entertainments of the Soul with God.* Birmingham, England: T. Holliwell, 1770.

Grou, John. *Manual for Interior Souls.* Translated from the French. 3rd ed. London: St. Anselm's Society, 1915.

[Harnett, Mary Vincent]. *The Life of Rev. Mother Catherine McAuley.* Edited by Richard Baptist O'Brien. Dublin: John F. Fowler, 1864.

Healy, Kathleen. *Frances Warde: American Founder of the Sisters of Mercy.* New York: Seabury Press, 1973.

Jeffery, Barbara. *Living for the Church before Everything Else: The Hardman Family Story.* N.p., n.d.

Kasper, Walter. *Mercy: The Essence of the Gospel and the Key to Christian Life,* translated by W. Madges. Mahwah, N.J.: Paulist Press, 2014.

Kelly, James, and Dáire Keogh, eds. *History of the Catholic Diocese of Dublin.* Dublin: Four Courts Press, 2000.

Kerr, Donal. "Dublin's Forgotten Archbishop: Daniel Murray, 1768–1852."

In *History of the Catholic Diocese of Dublin,* edited by James Kelly and Dáire Keogh, 247–67. Dublin: Four Courts Press, 2000.

Lash, Nicholas. *Theology for Pilgrims.* Notre Dame, Ind.: University of Notre Dame Press, 2008.

Lewis [Luis] de Granada. *The Sinner's Guide, in Two Books.* Translated from the Spanish. Philadelphia: Henry McGrath, [1844].

Liguori, Alphonsus M. *The True Spouse of Christ: or, The Nun Sanctified by the Virtues of Her State.* Translated from the Italian by a "Catholic Clergyman." Dublin: James Duffy, 1860.

———. *Visits to the Most Holy Sacrament.* Translated by N. Callan. Dublin: James Duffy, n.d.

Marin, Michel-Ange. *The Perfect Religious.* 1747. Translated from the French. Dublin: Repository of St. Mary's Asylum, 1845.

[Moore, Mary Clare, comp.]. *A Little Book of Practical Sayings, Advices and Prayers of Our Revered Foundress, Mother Mary Catharine [sic] McAuley.* London: Burns, Oates, 1868.

"Perfectae Caritatis: Decree on the Appropriate Renewal of the Religious Life." In *The Documents of Vatican II,* edited by Walter M. Abbott. New York: America Press, 1966.

Rahner, Karl. *Watch and Pray with Me.* Translated by William V. Dych. New York: Herder and Herder, 1966.

Rodriguez, Alonso. *The Practice of Christian and Religious Perfection.* Originally written in Spanish. Translated from the French copy of M. l'Abbé Regnier des Marais, of the Royal Academy of Paris. 3 vols. Kilkenny: John Reynolds, 1806.

Roker, Penny. "M. Mary Clare Moore, RSM." In *English Catholic Heroines,* edited by Joanna Bogle, 213–29. Leominster, England: Gracewing, 2009.

Sheldrake, Philip. *Spirituality and History: Questions of Interpretation and Method.* New York: Crossroad, 1991.

Sullivan, Mary C. "Catherine McAuley's Theological and Literary Debt to Alonso Rodriguez: The 'Spirit of the Institute' Parallels." *Recusant History* (now, *British Catholic History*) 20 (May 1990): 81–105.

———. *Catherine McAuley and the Tradition of Mercy.* Dublin: Four

Courts Press, 1995; Notre Dame, Ind.: University of Notre Dame Press, 1995. Cited as *CMcATM*.

———, ed. *The Correspondence of Catherine McAuley, 1818–1841*. Dublin: Four Courts Press, 2004; Washington: The Catholic University of America Press, 2004. Cited as *CCMcA*.

———, ed. *The Practical Sayings of Catherine McAuley*. Rochester, New York: Sisters of Mercy of the Americas, 2010. Reprint with new introduction of [Mary Clare Moore], comp. *A Little Book of the Practical Sayings, Advices, and Prayers of . . . Mary Catharine* [*sic*] *McAuley*. London: Burns, Oates, 1868.

———. *The Path of Mercy: The Life of Catherine McAuley*. Washington, D.C.: The Catholic University of America Press, 2012; Dublin: Four Courts Press, 2012.

Teresa of Avila. *The Complete Works of St. Teresa of Jesus*. Translated and edited by E. Allison Peers. Vol. 3. London: Sheed and Ward, 1946.

———. *The Collected Works of St. Teresa of Avila*. Translated by Kieran Kavanaugh and Otilio Rodriguez. 3 vols. Washington: Institute of Carmelite Studies, 1985.

Thomas à Kempis. *The Imitation of Christ*. Translated by R[ichard] Challoner. Dublin: Catholic Book Society, 1834.

Thomas of Jesus. *The Sufferings of our Lord Jesus Christ*. Translated from the Portuguese. 2 vols. Dublin: P. Wogan, 1794.

[Young, Ursula]. *The Soul United to Jesus in His Adorable Sacrament: or, Devout Methods of Hearing Mass before and after Communion*. London: Keating and Brown, 1821.

Index of Names

Index of Names

Index of Subjects

Index of Subjects

A Shining Lamp: The Oral Instructions of Catherine McAuley was designed in Arno by Kachergis Book Design of Pittsboro, North Carolina. It was printed on 60-pound House Natural Smooth and bound by Sheridan Books of Chelsea, Michigan.